the american
promise

the american promise
Equal Justice and Economic Opportunity

Edited by Arthur I. Blaustein

Transaction Books
New Brunswick (U.S.A.) and London (U.K.)

New material this edition copyright © 1982 by Transaction, Inc., New Brunswick, New Jersey 08903. Original edition published September 1981, National Advisory Council on Economic Opportunity, U.S. Government Printing Office.

Library of Congress Catalog Number: 81-16313
ISBN: 0-87855-905-1
Printed in the United States of America

Library of Congress Cataloging in Publication Data
Main entry under title:

The American promise.

1. Economic assistance, Domestic—United States.
2. Poor—United States.   I. Blaustein, Arthur I.
HC110.P63A715   338.973   81-16313
ISBN 0-87855-905-1   AACR2

TABLE OF CONTENTS

ACKNOWLEDGMENTS

The Council is particularly indebted to Dr. Robert Bellah, Dr. Elliott Currie, Diana Pearce, Harriette McAdoo and Dr. William M. Sullivan for their thoughtful contributions to this report.

The Council wishes to thank Kate Sieck and Kate Parkes of Berkeley, California, for their most helpful assistance; staff members Walter B. Quetsch and Dolores A. Washington; and particularly staff member Claudia P. Green for typing and preparing this manuscript for printing and distribution.

The Council also expresses its appreciation to Richard Rios, Lee Foley and Robert Landmann for their programmatic support.

MEMBERS OF THE NATIONAL ADVISORY COUNCIL ON ECONOMIC OPPORTUNITY

ARTHUR I. BLAUSTEIN, *Chairman*
Berkeley, Calif.

HANNAH H. BAIRD
Florence, Ky.

IRVING BLUESTONE
Detroit, Mich.

WILLIAM M. DALEY
Chicago, Ill.

L. C. DORSEY
Jackson, Miss.

HAZEL N. DUKES
Roslyn Heights, N.Y.

RUBY DUNCAN
Las Vegas, Nev.

GEOFFREY FAUX
Whitefield, Maine

EDWARD F. FEIGHAN
Cleveland, Ohio

LINDA HADLEY
Chinle, Navaho Nation
(Arizona)

JUAN J. MALDONADO
San Juan, Tex.

W. PHILIP MCLAURIN
Washington, D.C.

HENRY M. MESTRE, JR.
Oakland, Calif.

CHRISTINE PRATT-MARSTON
Lynnwood, Wash.

EVELYN WATTS
St. Petersburg, Fla.

Detailed biographies can be found in Appendix.

The Director of the Community Services Administration is an *ex officio* member of the Advisory Council.

We hold the moral obligation of
providing for old age, helpless
infancy, and poverty, is far
superior to that of supplying
the invented wants of courtly
extravagance.

THOMAS PAINE

Poverty is the great enemy of
human happiness; it certainly
destroys liberty and makes some
virtues impracticable, and
others extremely difficult.

SAMUEL JOHNSON

. . . Poverty—the most deadly
and prevalent of all diseases.

EUGENE O'NEILL

INTRODUCTION TO THE TRANSACTION EDITION

Arthur I. Blaustein *

In late March when the Council convened in Washington, D.C. for what were to become its final meetings, an air of depression and anxiety pervaded the deliberations. The discussion focused on the disturbing drift toward authoritarianism in our politics, our economics, and our social policy.

The Council's concern was punctuated by the realization that the incoming Administration seemed absolutely determined to punish its perceived enemies and to reward its acknowledged friends. The losers would be women, minorities, the young, the elderly, ordinary wage earners, and the poor—those segments of our society who had made modest gains in the past fifteen years as a direct result of Federal intervention and protection. The big winners would be wealthy individuals and corporations who had contributed heavily to the Reagan campaign. This apprehension was further aggravated by the growing awareness that those with power and wealth were actually claiming to be victimized by the poor, the real victims in our society.

Although we could not foretell the future, it was our common hope that the Reagan Administration would not push to its extreme a punitive and regressive public policy of using the poor as a scapegoat, for that would indeed signal a more rapid drift toward authoritarianism, a decline of moral values, and the disintegration of our national democratic processes.

The findings and recommendations of this *Report* are presented as a reasonable and constructive alternative to Administration premises, policies, and programs. It is offered not only with conviction but as a challenge, one which suggests that no American can say, "I didn't know what was happening, how it happened, or whether we had any choice." We always have a choice.

---

*Mr. Blaustein was appointed Chairman of the National Advisory Council on Economic Opportunity by President Jimmy Carter in August of 1977. He was reappointed for a three-year term in August, 1980. The Council, which has served five Presidents since 1965, was abolished on September 30, 1981, by the Reagan Administration.

The Council's Task

Two unrelated incidents shaped the direction of this *Report*; each occurred about three years ago. The first involved a Council colleague who was assisting local groups interested in organizing fuel cooperatives in his home state of Maine. That winter was unusually cold and the price of home heating oil had tripled since the 1974 OPEC jolt, placing an enormous financial burden on the average family in this state with its extremely low per capita income.

He was invited to make a presentation to about 200 residents in a town church, where one of the "Happy Guys" television reporters from Portland baited a farmer after the talk asking, "What do you think of this outside agitation?" The farmer, who was about 70, paused for a moment and, with an edge of flint in his voice, said, "You know, I'm a fourth-generation Republican Yankee—just like my father, my grandfather and my great-grandfather—but if I've learned anything, it's that there are two kinds of politics and economics in America. The first kind is what I see on television and what politicians tell me when they want my vote. The other kind is what me and my friends talk about over doughnuts and coffee. And that's what this young fellow was talking about tonight—and he made a lot of sense to me."

The second incident occurred while I was watching "Bill Moyers' Journal." Moyers was interviewing Robert Penn Warren, whom *Newsweek* recently called "the dean of American letters." Moyers said, "Sir, you are one of America's leading writers, a poet, an historian, and a philosopher. Can you tell me how we can resolve the terrible crises that surround us: our cities are decaying, our health care is atrocious, we have terrible crises in education, transportation, housing, and energy. There is still much poverty..."

Mr. Warren paused, leaned forward, and said, "Well, Bill, for a beginning, I think it would be good if we would stop lying to one another."

Thus in outlining an agenda during the course of the Council's deliberations I had a modest vision, but it was a very clear one: we would prepare a report that would deal with the most compelling issues of our time, and they would be presented in a direct, cogent, and readable manner. The report would not be theoretical or abstract, nor would it hide behind bureaucratic jargon; it would strike a reasonable balance between facts, statistics, theories, and real-life circumstances. And it would expose false myths, rhetoric, deceit, and official lying. We assumed that most Americans share a common goal: how do we as a nation achieve a stable, equitable, and democratic society that does not suffer from inflations, depressions, unemployment, gross waste of human and national resources, and the grinding misery of poverty. In short, we wanted a report that could be read by ordinary Americans; it would be the kind that could be discussed over coffee and doughnuts.

That the mass media are inadequate to inform the public on the most crucial issues of our time is a matter of record. Human services—well-built, low-cost housing; decent health care; affordable energy; better mass transportation; nutrition; neighborhood development; economic revitalization; care for the elderly; and meaningful jobs—are no match for mass media that cannot sate themselves enough with a daily, and morbid, bombardment of murders, accidents, fires, floods, bombings, scandals, assaults, or the standard fare of gossip about those afforded celebrity status. As *People*'s headline for its story on Chevy Chase put it, "He's Hot and You're Not." To say that there is a vacuum of substance in the mass communications industry in America today—whose bottom line is "either you are a star or a nobody"—is all too obvious. An important task of the Council, we felt, was to serve as a conscience and remind all of us that everyone, even the poorest American, is a somebody.

The Reagan Revolution

On October 1 the Reagan Economic Recovery Program took effect. The program itself is revolutionary in that it: signifies a radical departure from the public policies of the past fifty years; embraces an economic theory that is untried; changes the nature of the relationship between the Federal government and individual citizens; and will, in some way, affect the lives of all Americans.

Many elements of this program, taken separately, are highly questionable. For example, "supply-side" economics and monetarism are contradictory, much like getting on an elevator and pressing the up and down buttons simultaneously, hoping to go both ways at once. But the President has done a remarkable job of selling a "supply-side" theory that, like any theory, cannot be proved or disproved in the abstract. The real test will come soon enough in the practical application.

Of far more critical importance, though, is a fundamental assumption that underlies the larger policy formulation. This assumption is so flawed and ill-conceived that it seriously jeopardizes any prospects for the success of the whole venture. It is the illusion that economic policy can be separated from social policy. This is impossible, and the consequences of believing it are grave. By separating economic theory from social policy and pursuing the former at the expense of the latter, the Administration has adopted a strategy of brinksmanship that could lead to social chaos. Drastic cuts in basic social and human service programs will exact social and human costs, and they will also appear as direct financial costs at future times in different ledgers.

There is a very real price to be paid for the reduction of human and social services. The price is that these cutbacks will not reduce crime; they will increase it. They will not reduce drug abuse; they will increase it. They will not reduce physical and mental illness; they will increase it.

They will not promote better family life; they will destabilize it. They will not reduce alcoholism; they will increase it. They will not increase respect for the law; they will weaken it. These painful realities have not been factored into the Administration's game plan.

At present, there exists an air of suspended disbelief over the radical changes of the past six months. That is because the layoffs, shutdowns, cutbacks, and reduced paychecks have just begun. The day of reckoning, October 1, 1981, will be remembered as a day of infamy, for it will mark the beginning of the worst massacre of social and human service programs in American history. As a direct result of these policies more than four million ordinary working Americans will probably be reduced to poverty in the first full year of the Reagan economic plan (October 1, 1981–September 30, 1982); that is, if David Stockman and the Office of Management and Budget do not deliberately attempt to change the standards and criteria for measuring poverty in order to cover up this human catastrophe and further deceive the American people. This will mark the largest single-year jump in poverty for over forty years, since the Great Depression.

The four particular elements of the Administration's program that threaten to undermine our social equilibrium are: (1) the massive across-the-board cuts in social and human service programs; (2) the transfer of Federal authority and program responsibility to the states through block grant programs; (3) the tax cuts, which are regressive in that they are unfair to the middle class and the poor; and (4) the abolition of delivery systems provided for in the Economic Opportunity Act and the Legal Services Corporation Act.

For the more than 29 million poor Americans, and another 30 million nearly-poor, each of these decisions taken alone would be painful, but taken together they will be devastating. In addition to widespread human suffering, the budget cuts will undermine two basic tenets of the Reagan philosophy: the work ethic and family life. From an Administration that places high priority on the importance of family life and the work ethic, this budget will be self-defeating; these policies will actually encourage welfare dependency instead of work, family breakdown instead of family stability.

The Administration's contention that renewed economic growth will eventually "trickle down" to the poor to offset the loss of social programs flies in the face of everything we know about poverty today. The best research indicates the opposite, that growth in the private economy has had a declining role in reducing poverty, and that virtually all of the reduction in poverty since the mid-1960's has been brought about through expansion of social insurance and income-transfer programs of the kind now under attack by the Administration.

The stubborn persistence of poverty in the face of economic growth results in part from the changing nature of the poverty population. What has occurred is the creation of a "new" poor, a population whom the private economy has passed by. Even in good times the new poor—the elderly, the disabled, disadvantaged youth, women heading families with small children—are rarely hired by the private sector, despite all the want ads the President keeps telling us about. In 1978, a year of economic recovery, the unemployment rate among disadvantaged minority youth was 41 percent.

Because few of the new poor can be absorbed into the private economy without special assistance and support, the massive suffering these program cuts will bring cannot be balanced by any credible long-range benefits from the Administration's program—even under the most optimistic economic assumptions. Instead, any economic renewal resulting from the Administration's policies would take place at the expense of stable, rewarding family lives and genuine work opportunities for the poor.

In addition to the massive cuts, the decision to turn over to the states as block grants specific social, educational, and health (categorical) programs, which have been the responsibility of the Federal government, raises serious institutional problems as to whether or not basic human and social services can be adequately provided.

The economic difficulties facing our nation are complex and often seem overwhelming, but these difficulties cannot be used as an excuse for reneging on our social and moral commitments as a nation. The notion that national issues—ones that require national policy and programs and that are a part of our national purpose—should suddenly devolve to the states because someone, almost as an afterthought or rationalization, discovers state sovereignty, is shallow and irresponsible. The issue is not Federal versus State; rather, it is the diminution or avoidance of any national standards of responsibility and accountability. To deflect, suspend, or fragment responsibility and accountability suggests that we are either renouncing or failing to assert our moral purpose as a nation. Worse than that, the Administration seems to be denying that this moral purpose exists.

In essence, the effect of the Administration's block grant program is to destroy existing support systems that are effective, that have a proven capacity to deliver services, and that utilize local planning and implementation capabilities. What they are being replaced with is an inequitable system that has a poor track record; that is restrictively financed, more bureaucratic, and less accountable; and that is subject to intense political pressures. The last point is extremely important in that effective and efficient use of limited federal funds is being sacrificed to conflicting political interests in each state. Instead of the more efficient government that Mr. Reagan promises, we will have fifty bureaucratic and anachronistic messes: government by provisional catastrophe.

What is also disturbing is the ideological implication behind present economic policies, in that it departs from the genuine conservative leadership that has played such an important role in American history.

Historically, promises of lower taxes and economic privatism have never been central issues. Traditionally, conservative leaders have focused primarily on underlying problems of the human community—issues of leadership, of equality of opportunity, of continuity and order, of the obligations of the strong to the weak, and of the safeguards needed to keep the privileged from abusing their power.

The Real Problems

The *Report* focuses on five aspects of American social, economic, and political life that directly affect the poor, and indirectly affect us all:

- the problems of unemployment and inflation;
- the problems of women in poverty;
- the implementation of national antipoverty policies through appropriate delivery systems;
- the myths of poverty; and
- the role of voluntary associations, the meaning of civic responsibility, and the shared values of our society at large.

The *Report* goes on to explore the issue of the moral values so fundamental to the well-being of our country. For one of the greatest difficulties we face as a nation seeking to eliminate poverty is our view of the problem itself—which gets at the basic attitudes and moral values underlying social, political, and economic realities.

In his encyclical, "Redeemer of Man," Pope John Paul II expressed a special concern for social and economic justice and the human suffering caused by poverty. In calling for a new commitment to social and moral values, John Paul II said:

> We have before us a great drama that can leave nobody indifferent. The person who, on the one hand, is trying to draw the maximum profit and, on the other hand, is paying the price in damage and injury is always man. The drama is made still worse by the presence close at hand of the privileged social classes and of the rich countries, which accumulate goods to an excessive degree. Add to this the fever of inflation and the plague of unemployment—these are further symptoms of the moral disorder.

Fearing the drift toward social disintegration, we raised some fundamental issues of human concern in this *Report*, issues directed at the crucial economic and social paradoxes cited by the Pope.

The Council unanimously agreed on the importance of providing a historical context for American values and beliefs, to better understand the relationship and the conflicts between material and spiritual values.

First we asked ourselves: What are the ambiguities inherent in these conflicts? Why do Americans, who are so rich in material advantages, still feel alienation, a lack of connectedness to the self and their community, and despair over the future?

One reason, we decided, is that as a nation we seem to have lost the ability to identify with either a sense of history or a belief in the continuity of shared positive values. To some extent, we have even lost our ability to recognize and agree on those values. Our alienation and despair come, then, from a haunting, all-but-forgotten knowledge that material gifts and surface satisfactions cannot substitute for stability, dignity, integrity, and the ability to value.

Robert Penn Warren, on his recent 75th birthday, dealt with the same problems. He said: "History is dying . . . . [If] this country loses its sense of history, it has lost its sense to complicate men's feelings and emotions. If I could, I would re-evaluate the education system in this country, to emphasize history and literature." Warren gets to the heart of the issue: that the values of a society are determined by connectedness to a history and the cultural values passed on through its literature. He perceives that substituting recently acquired quantitative measures of success—acquisition, aggressiveness, consuming—has disrupted our historical tradition of qualitative values—citizen participation, public interest, cooperation, and a self-worth defined by character and integrity.

Although I fully agree with Mr. Warren's perceptions, I do not believe that our educational system can do the job alone. It simply cannot compete with the overload of a mass media that assaults us day and night with a totally different set of messages undercutting both our values and our traditions. The discipline of education is no match for the passivity of entertainment. In this conflict, there are two kinds of light: the glow that illumines and the glare that obscures, and the latter seems to be winning a losing battle—the loss being that learning is stultified, that growth is stunted, and that we seek simplistic answers to complex problems.

The Council's historical review and insights into the "myths of poverty" followed by an analysis of available options reduce the larger problem to two basic conflicts: public versus private interest, and qualitative versus quantitative values. For example, there is general agreement that we urgently need to stabilize our economy. To do so requires common acceptance and understanding of the structural economic problems of concurrent inflation and recession. It is crucial, then, that *all* segments of society, including the private sector, cooperate in a national effort based on trust and compromise. If we assume that government's effort is reasonably equitable, it then follows that the private sector will temper its demands in order to help alleviate our national crisis. Yet this is just not happening.

Why not? One has only to open a magazine or newspaper or turn on radio or television to be assaulted by antigovernment advertisements financed by big business political action committees (PACs). Prior to Reagan's election, they depicted all public employees as bungling fools. They spent untold millions to say that the undeserving poor, with the help of government, had brought on our economic ills, so we need only tighten *their* belts (i.e., eliminate human and social services) and all would be well again. They, the deserving affluent, and the big oil companies, defense contractors, banks, and real estate developers, would not have to even think of tightening *their* belts. The message is slickly packaged in hypnotically stunning layouts and cinematography, lucrative messages that the mass media eagerly repeat editorially. So the spirit of California's Proposition 13 has spread, eroding public trust in government and destroying the atmosphere vital to healthy cooperation among all segments of society.

Two years ago, in speaking to a group of business executives, George Gallup said: "The 1980's probably will be marked by turmoil, unpleasantness and civil strife . . . a moral crisis of the first dimension . . . severe dislocation in society. . . . [B]ecause of unemployment and the serious crowded ghetto situation, it can only go one way." These social and economic pressures persist in America today despite all the earlier findings and warnings of "blue ribbon" Presidential Commissions, including the McCone, Kerner, Scranton, Breathitt, and Eisenhower Commissions. Gallup only echoes their conclusions that the problems are national in scope and that the Federal government must focus on the *causes* of poverty: inadequate health care, impaired education, lack of job opportunities, deteriorating housing, and decaying neighborhoods. Nothing has occurred in the past two years to dispute the findings and recommendations of these earlier commissions. And the predictions of Gallup become more probable as the Federal government abdicates its responsibility. There is a role for the private sector, for private charities, and for the states, but only the Federal government can provide the political, economic, social, and moral leadership.

A Short History—The War on Poverty

In 1965 we began to seriously fight these root causes of poverty. For over fifteen years Americans have demonstrated their commitment, openness, and generosity. President Lyndon Johnson and Congress in 1965 initiated legislation that gave us such programs as Head Start, Legal Services, Foster Grandparents, VISTA, Community Action Agencies (CAAs), and Community Economic Development Corporations (CDCs). These programs were direct and specific, aimed at pressing local problems. Young and old, professionals and disadvantaged, together developed their potential through truly needed participation in community life. It was a time of idealism and enthusiasm, when doctors, lawyers, teachers, accountants, nurses, engineers, and grandparents gave of themselves. I believe that the rediscovery of this spirit would be the most salutary response possible to cope with our present social and economic problems. We need not suffer from a crisis of will; the problems are not insolvable when people are determined to resolve them.

In reviewing the policies of the past two decades, we have seen various strategies and theories come and go—a welfare-reform strategy, a private-sector jobs strategy, a minority-entrepreneurship strategy, a special-revenue strategy. Yet I believe that if we had never passed the original legislation, the Economic Opportunity Act of 1964, which created an independent Federal agency supporting CAAs (and CDCs in 1967), we would have to invent it today. It created the only delivery mechanisms—imperfect as they may be—that relate policies and programs to people. That is the genuine achievement of the Economic Opportunity Act. Lost in the clichés, slogans, and double-talk of anti-government rhetoric are the solid accomplishments. The value of these programs, services, and innovations has been obscured; the extraordinary contributions have been slighted.

The Nixon Administration in 1969 reversed this direction and we had to contend with a hostile political climate that pervaded our public life. It replaced action with benign neglect, sapped our good intentions, and clouded our judgment and memory of traditional values, to the detriment of real progress on any of these vitally necessary programs.

The Carter Administration attempted to refocus attention on human and social priorities but was overwhelmed by a combination of high inflation and political negativism, the latter a highly sophisticated propaganda campaign waged by the New Right and financed by corporate political action committees.

The "politics of negativism" is perpetuated by a vicious cycle fueled by a "get tough" campaign (a prominent part of Proposition 13 fever) in which reactionary politicians feed the media their own self-serving attacks on social programs. Next in the cycle are the mass media, eager to pass these attacks on to the public along with the commercial ads of the private sector (described above) that further confuse and condition with antigovernment sloganeering. The circle closes when well-heeled lobbyists for privileged interests return the politicians' messages to them, so reinforcing the body of mythology, half-truths, and distortions.

Who are the subjects of these attacks? Unemployed young people in CETA programs, mental patients, elderly people on fixed incomes, single-parent mothers dependent on day care and Food Stamps, owners of small family farms, handicapped persons needing special education, and blue-collar workers unable to afford soaring hospital and housing costs. We still seem to suffer a hangover from the "Nixonization" era: a period of spitefulness, nastiness, fear, and deceit—an era that officially condoned and even encouraged negative attitudes, code words, and symbols directed against the poor in particular, and toward basic human and social service programs in general.

Whatever their intentions or self-delusions, those who build reputations by attacking the most powerless elements of our society are cowards. Not surprisingly, they moralize endlessly over the illness: the "problems" of mental breakdown, alcoholism, drug abuse, suicide, child and spouse abuse, and disrupted families, but they have no heart for the rigorous thought and work of finding cures, or even just relieving some of the symptoms. And, bullies and hypocrites that they are, they identify sympathetically with the Hunt family and its cash-flow difficulty in cornering the silver market, but not with the Jones family and its difficulty in coping with the problems of living on a budget that calls for spending 110 percent of its income to keep up with the costs of basic necessities—food, shelter, health care, and energy.

Politics today, in a period of limited economic growth, seems to have reached a level of abstractedness that removes it from the commonplace circumstances of ordinary Americans. When a sane and civilized family runs into tough financial times, two things happen. The one thing that they *do* do is to assure that those members of the family who are least able to fend for themselves are given the protection and minimum amenities necessary for survival. The one thing that they *do not* do is to allow those who have more than enough and are enjoying luxuries to continue to hoard. There *are* certain natural principles of behavior, of caring and decency, that have prior claim over untested game plans of economic theorists or politicians on the make. It is the adherence to these principles that defines us as human.

A War Against the Poor

The Reagan Administration, despite its early pledges to provide a "safety net" for the "truly needy," has in fact adopted policies that amount to a war against the poor. The tax and budget cuts—the Reagan economic plan—are in reality a carnival for wealthy speculators and hell on earth for the poor, with the middle class still being squeezed. The cuts were not made in order to balance the budget; they were simply massive transfers from social programs to pay for new weapon systems. Moreover, this was accomplished in a policy vacuum. The Administration has not provided the American people with a strategic definition as to how this excessive arms build-up fits into our larger defense or foreign policy. Is it in the national interest to relegate our most precious assets—our human and natural resources—to the junkpile, while we increase the stockpiling of weapons of mass destruction in an arms race where overkill has long been achieved?

The steady drumbeat of rhetoric emanating from Administration officials and shrewdly orchestrated by the White House is intended to create, and has heretofore succeeded in creating, a counter-reality and new myths with respect to social policy. For example, by continuously referring to economic opportunity and equal justice programs as *welfare* programs, the Administration has misled the American public. (The corollary to this myth, which also contributes to public misunderstanding, is that "these programs are only for minorities." This is untrue, as two-thirds of the poor in America are white.) These programs are in fact designed to achieve the opposite: to create jobs and economic opportunities and to encourage people dependent upon welfare to become productive citizens and taxpayers. By seeking to eliminate these programs and substituting its own policies, the Administration will deny upward mobility to millions on welfare and will force many of the working poor into welfare dependency. By transferring huge amounts of funds from human and social programs to the Pentagon, the Administration is not dampening inflation, it is fueling it.

In order to gain support for its economic package, the Administration, through David Stockman, has conjured up the specter of an "economic Dunkirk." Instead, what is actually being perpetrated is a "social Pearl Harbor," which will have a devastating impact on the defenseless poor. It will also wipe out the modest gains made in the past fifteen years by women, the elderly, minorities, and the young—the most vulnerable segments of our society.

Similarly, it is hard to imagine what goes through the heads of politicians opposed to the CETA Public Service Employment Program. Their criticism, whether from a social, political, economic, or cost-accountability viewpoint, is patently absurd. The only real choice is whether our society believes it of greater value to keep a youngster in a state prison at an annual cost of $14,000, in a drug rehabilitation center for $17,000, in a mental institution for over $20,000, *or* to develop job-training and job-creating programs at $7,000 to $9,000. We do not need a crash course in zero-base budgeting or human relations to know that all but the last course are wasteful and destructive to society and its individual members.

The vast majority of Federal programs being abolished, curtailed, or turned over to the states have helped promote racial and ethnic cooperation. They have helped overcome the physical despair and isolation of the rural poor. They have been instrumental in targeting resources and delivering comprehensive services.

That they have helped to allay the anxiety of the urban poor is a matter of public record. Conditions, bad as they are, could have worsened. These programs have been the catalysts to force state and local governments to stop sweeping malicious and discriminatory practices under the rug, and so have relieved tensions and reduced disillusionments. They have opened new potentials in health care, education, nutrition, housing, job development, the law, weatherization, migrant labor, day care, and consumer protection. There have been some mistakes, but they are minuscule compared to the concrete achievements.

With limited resources and often in a hostile political environment, these programs have carried the burden of keeping the promise and conscience of this nation alive. Such programs must be expanded, not abolished.

National Leadership and Moral Values

If we abolish crucial programs, we will destroy all their valuable achievements as well. And then what happens? Rather than engage in a national effort based on trust and compromise, rather than pursue the difficult choice of maintaining moral standards and national purpose—must we revert to our basest instincts, which in turn would allow us to exploit our conflicts and encourage us always to take the easy choice? Look out for number one; those who can't are shiftless, a drag on the economy. Our moral decline deepens as we are tempted to choose quantity over quality, greed over sharing, and privilege over human needs; as we condone the sheer political force of special and self-serving private interests over the legitimate public authority that represents our nation's best interests.

Rather than activism, idealism, equality, and vitality, the Reagan prescription for economic recovery amounts to apathy, fatalism, inequality, passivity, and acquiescence; and human needs become subordinated to technical arrogance. People programs are out and tax avoidance schemes are in.

Jacob Bronowski, the distinguished scientist, shed light on this conflict when he said: "We have to cure ourselves of the itch for absolute knowledge and power. We have to close the distance between the push-button order and the human act. We have to touch people." This thought goes back to the earlier point regarding the crucial importance of continuing education. In addition to our traditional educational institutions, voluntary associations have an absolutely critical role to perform, in that they too must become involved in the process of adult civic education at the community level.

That is in essence what Abraham Lincoln meant when he continuously reminded us that our primary task as a nation should be to teach and reteach American political history. He was deeply concerned lest we forget the pain and struggle that were so much a part of our unique historical experience. For Lincoln, there was no higher calling than that of striving to preserve a "public liberty" that would promote the common good. Which is, of course, the opposite of the contemporary notion of private interest for personal gain.

It all comes down to what Robert Penn Warren expressed so well, the great loss we suffer when we break with our historical and literary traditions. A society is shaped and defined by the myths and symbols it adheres to and which it conveys to its young. These myths and symbols also play a significant role in determining the priorities of our political economy and the way we respond to social problems—in that they determine our habits, attitudes, manners, tastes, and prejudices. These cultural patterns, in turn, either serve to enhance or undermine our moral sensibility, social consciousness, political awareness, economic behavior, and ethical perceptions, all of which are parts of that whole that forms our national character. And our national character both determines and reflects those policies, programs, and priorities that define who we are as a nation and a people.

Yet when we look around today we find our lives dominated by false symbols and myths related to superstars and superbowls: *Jaws* and *Star Wars*, TV commercials and "gossipy" journalism, Valium and junk food, drugs and discos, gimmicks and gadgets, and a technology of speed and efficiency that neither questions its means nor knows its ends. In the past thirty years, with the advent of new mass marketing and advertising techniques, we have experienced an entirely new phenomenon in America. It is the acceptance of the notion that there is no human impulse—no matter how neurotic, anxiety-producing, or destructive—that cannot be turned into a commodity just to make a buck. We may chew our nails and look for hidden meanings or answers, but the wastelands, the hollowness, and the alienation are still the end result of our own passive acceptance of this antihuman notion, the demoralizing pursuit of mindless consumerism.

We have allowed ourselves to be cut off from our own history—a rich tradition, a hope, a vitality, a true celebration of America; that of the real-life myths and symbols conveyed by our great American literary tradition. From the struggle for social freedom, the wonderment of our potential, and the democratic visions of Herman Melville, James Fenimore Cooper, Ralph Waldo Emerson, Henry David Thoreau, Mark Twain, Walt Whitman, Edwin Arlington Robinson, Emily Dickinson, and Willa Cather, to the modern social and economic realism of Hart Crane, Edith Wharton, F. Scott Fitzgerald, Theodore Dreiser, William Faulkner, Ernest Hemingway, Carl Sandburg, Langston Hughes, Robert Frost, John Steinbeck, Carson McCullers, Joyce Carol Oates, Joseph Heller, E.L. Doctorow, John Nichols, and Ralph Ellison—our literary historians have deliberately and painfully tried to make us aware of the ironic complications and tragic consequences of depersonalization and dehumanization.

There is in the American sensibility a sense of belief and a commitment to action; a logical connection—both symbolic and real—between the megalomania of Captain Ahab and the search for dignity, freedom, and identity of Ellison's *The Invisible Man*. The consequences of denying this awareness and sensibility are dismay, chaos, and fragmentation. Without an awareness of the depersonalization and dehumanization processes, we can only succumb to the tragic undertones.

In one sense all of today's problems are richly preserved by these literary historians, our nation's "unelected legislators," for they are the eternal problems of the human condition. If we choose to ignore the past, we are condemned to repeat our mistakes. If we fail to heed the warnings of the civil disorders of the sixties, we will be inviting more outbursts like the more recent one in Miami, for the pent-up frustration and seething anger that exist in most other poor communities throughout America are very real. In Miami, we heard the painful cry of smothered human aspirations. If we choose to accept and learn from our past we will confront the underlying conflicts that touch the very soul of our society, and by acting on this knowledge we can provide positive solutions and unifying themes that will enliven our spirit as a nation.

In this sense, our political and literary history has provided us with a common-sense vision of the American promise that calls for justice, freedom, equality, and opportunity. We may forget or we may deny, but we cannot change our historical legacy. The uniqueness of our nation is that the "noble experiment" was a quest to enhance the human condition, to enrich democratic values, to ensure the general welfare, and to endure against adversity.

I am well aware that it is quite unfashionable in these days of "getting the government off our back" slogans to speak of more qualitative initiatives from government. To put it bluntly, this Administration is pandering to, and exploiting, the most regressive and antisocial tendencies in our national character. They are undermining trust in the ability of the one force, government, that has the potential to balance, secure, and protect the freedoms and liberties of *all* our people, and to balance public and private interests. A vital and healthy Federal government is indispensable to the well-being and sovereignty of a self-governing people. That is, after all, what democracy is all about. Without this protection, whole segments of our society—especially those who can least afford it—will give up hope, will become more frustrated and alienated; and this can only serve to further undermine the very social fabric of all our communities.

During our bicentennial year, I took the opportunity to reread Jefferson, Madison, Hamilton, and the *Federalist Papers*, and recalled that our founding fathers were well aware that politics and economics were interrelated faces of power, each necessitating its own checks and balances. What impressed me most, though, was their mature leadership, one that had a clear and qualitative vision of the "public interest." And one that was based on a genuine commitment to social and political equality as well as to economic opportunity. It is my belief that a commitment to this sense of public interest is just as important today.

Finally, it must be said in response to the downgrading of national commitment that only those people have a future, and only those people can be called humane and historic, who have an intuitive sense of what is important and significant in both their national and public institutions, and who value them. It is this conviction and the continuing belief in the common-sense vision of the American promise that demand that we begin a serious dialogue over economic and social policies. This is absolutely essential to the democratic process. The

Reagan Administration's radical and dangerous changes have, in violation of this necessity, occurred without any serious national debate. Mr. Reagan seems to think that his electoral "mandate" has changed our government from a representative democracy to a royal monarchy.

For the past six months there has been an unconscious cynicism in the way the mass media have reported the previous day's happenings: REAGAN WINS AGAIN or HOUSE DEMS BEATEN. The political life of the country has been reduced to little more than a struggle for political power, the results not unlike the score of a football game. There seems to be no higher good, no national purpose, no critical judgment.

Reaganomics, as well as the Administration's overt antisocial political policies, are not based on a commitment to any higher principles such as freedom, liberty, equality, justice, or opportunity, although pieties are mouthed at the drop of a camera. The Administration's policies instead are based on the very narrow personal prejudices and biases of a group of men who have been motivated by the acquisition of money and power and who have a contempt for human sensibilities. The intellectual firmament from whence the policies spring—the writings and doodlings of George Gilder and Arthur Laffer—are self-serving and pretentious. Both Gilder and Laffer seem to have constructed a hypothesis to fit a simple notion: "The status quo is good to me, so I'll be good to the status quo." It is a sorry combination of the theory of the leisure class and the leisure of the theory class.

Everyone says, "Give them a chance." For the past eight months I have listened carefully to the President, I have heard the explanations of his chief advisers, and I have read about the frenetic changes wrought by the New Right. All of it has reminded me of a passage in "The Heart of Darkness." Joseph Conrad put it this way:

> Their talk was the talk of sordid buccaneers: it was reckless without hardihood, greedy without audacity, and cruel without courage; there was not an atom of foresight . . . in the whole batch of them, and they did not seem aware these things are wanted for the work of the world.

These words fit the conservative frenzy in Washington; they contain the mood and the moral nullity of the reactionary enterprise that seeks to tear apart the public good. It is almost as though the thought never occurred to the Administration that it is impossible for a country to sustain itself, much less to mature, on a fare of smiling one-liners, rerun ideas, hot-house theories, paranoia, and a social policy based on a hostile notion that seems to say, "Let them eat jellybeans."

October 30,1981
Berkeley, California

PREFACE

Twenty years ago, one of our nation's most eminent thinkers, Archibald MacLeish, paid tribute to the pioneering work of another American leader of his time, Jane Addams. The Council believes that it is worthwhile to include this work in the Preface because it raises two very basic and important contemporary issues.

MacLeish places the first issue in perspective by saying:

> We talk as though the great question before our society was whether the things that need to be done in America to keep this last best hope of earth alive should be done by the federal government or by the states or perhaps by the cities or by industries or by some other kind of organization. But that, of course, is not the question. The question before our society is simply whether or not those things *will* be *done*.

The second issue posed by MacLeish is more general, but no less fundamental. He asks whether or not we as individuals, or as a nation through our national policies, should take an active or passive role in dealing with the most pressing social issues of our time, including that of poverty in America. And that question, most certainly, is about to be decided by Congress in the coming months.

In 1964, the President and Congress respectively asked for and enacted the Economic Opportunity Act, which specifically called for new initiatives and an active role for the Federal Government in seeking to alleviate the problems of the poor. This year, President Reagan, through his economic package and budget requests, has made the decision to reverse direction by not seeking re-authorization authority for the Economic Opportunity Act and the Legal Services Corporation Act. The Council believes this is an extremely critical decision. For reasons outlined in this *Report*, we must go on record as being vigorously opposed to such action. The Council is asking the President to reconsider his decision, and we recommend that Congress extend the Economic Opportunity Act, and the Legal Services Corporation Act, for three years.

In the essay that follows, we think that Mr. MacLeish puts these critical issues into a thoughtful perspective.

Jane Addams of Chicago
November 21, 1960

Robert Frost, who has, as all the world knows, a genius for

putting unsayable things in wry simplicities, found precisely the word for our view of what lies ahead when he was asked, at the dedication of the Seagram Building in New York, to talk about the future. "I don't," said Mr. Frost, "*advocate* it." And neither do the rest of us. When we look ahead we see nothing but impossible alternatives—slavery of soul on the one hand, death of body on the other. Nothing beckons us. Where there is not malice there are lies, where there is not dogmatism of one kind there is dogmatism of another, . . . where the mind is still free the heart is afraid. There is a shadow across the whole prospect ahead which we call the shadow of the bomb but which may well be the shadow of our own fear or of our own failure. The old men are glad they will not have to cross into that country while the young men shy away, double back, hunt for hatchways leading underground, and the rest of us sleep-walk forward, our eyes and ears closed to everything but the hum of the new deep freeze and the lilt of the singing commercials. We don't blame ourselves for this—rather we pity ourselves. And certainly we never compare ourselves to our disadvantage with that earlier and braver generation. Theirs, after all, we say, was a simpler time when it was easy to be brave—no bomb—no Communism—no worldwide religious war. Jane Addams's Chicago was the great, brawling, burly, bustling Chicago of Carl Sandburg's early poems—a city that was going somewhere in a country that was going somewhere in a world that was watching with envious awe. There was nothing to fight in those days but crooked politicians and goons and gangsters. The future was possible then—more than possible—a promise. you could walk toward the future as you walked toward the Lake. It was there.

But was it? To us that future is the past: we can afford to be confident about it. But how did it look to the men and women who saw it ahead of them? Were they as comfortable with Carl Sandburg's poems as we are who know them so well we take them for granted? It is true Jane Addams's generation had no ingenious suicidal invention to worry about but it had killers of its own—humbler in status and more modest in murderousness but no less lethal for that: filthy milk, foul sanitation, rotting garbage, miserable schools, all of them aided and abetted by political corruption and social indifference.

To look back now into the world of the Pullman Strike, of the Altgeld controversy, of the fight over factory legislation, of the invalidation by the state Supreme Court of the eight-hour law for women, of the fight against clean milk legislation, is to look into a black night of American reaction which might well have seemed as hopeless to Jane Addams. . . .

Blacker perhaps, because she had so few beside her who thought it was black. We have friends in our darkness. The best minds of our generation are with us. A few, in France particularly, may have drifted across to the side of night but only to drift back again when they woke to where they were. But it was not so with Jane Addams. The decent and responsible opinion of her time was either against her or indifferent to the issue she raised. It was not a crank who said that Jane Addams ought to be hanged to the nearest lamp post: it was a solid citizen who, like other solid citizens, regarded any legislation aimed at the protection of children in factories as an attack on his right, as a citizen of a free country, to do as he pleased. And it was not an irresponsible newspaper which hounded her as a radical: it was a newspaper most of the responsible people of the city read.

I know, I think, what I am talking about. My father who came to Chicago as a Scots boy of eighteen in 1856 became one of the responsible men of the city. He was the founder, though not the owner, of one of the city's principal businesses. He was one of the founders of the University of Chicago and for many years vice-president of its board of trustees. He was one of the most respected men in his church. He was high-minded in the precise and literal sense of that term, scrupulous in his relations with others, generous even when he could not afford generosity—a just man and a fair man. Above all he was a man just and fair in his relations with his employees as he understood those relations. And yet one of my earliest memories of my father is a memory of a burst of anger—they were rare for he had mastered his tongue—occasioned by the beginnings of trade union organization in Chicago. And he was not, of course, alone in that anger. On the contrary he was milder in it and certainly less vociferous than most of the employers of labor whom Jane Addams knew.

It does not require, I think, an unusual effort of imagination to realize that the future must have looked about as dark at the turn of the century to a woman who believed what Jane Addams believed as it looks now to men and women who believe what we believe. Nor does it require unusual powers of discrimination to perceive that one difference between Jane Addams's generation and ours was her unwillingness, and the unwillingness of her friends, to be frightened by that darkness. But that is not the sole difference between us. There is also another. Not only did Jane Addams and her friends *dare* the future: they dared it *themselves*. From the moment when Jane Addams, after her doubting and questioning in her own country and abroad, stumbled upon that auction of rotting vegetables in a London slum—from the moment when her "idea" crystallized at Toynbee Hall in Whitechapel—she saw her life ahead as something *she* must *do*. Hull House was not a house: it was an action—a young woman's action—a personal action undertaken on the basis of a personal experience and a personal decision.

Anyone who does not understand that fact does not understand her history. On that first trip of hers to Europe Jane Addams wrote that "somewhere in the process of being educated" the first generation of "college women" to which she saw herself belonging "had lost that simple and almost automatic response to the human appeal—that old healthful reaction resulting in *activity* in the mere presence of suffering or of helplessness." *She* had not lost that response nor had those others who joined her at Polk and Halsted streets. They were not trained social workers: there were no trained social workers in our sense of the phrase in 1889. They were not even students, in any formal sense, of sociology. There was no department of sociology in any American university until one was established at Chicago in 1892. But unprepared and inexperienced as these women were they nevertheless set about to do *themselves* what they were persuaded had to be done. And it is there that they differ most dramatically from us.

We are so accustomed to have specialists of one kind or another live our lives for us that it rarely crosses our minds that we might at least *attempt* to live them for ourselves. We complain—particularly here within reach of the Voice from the Tribune Tower—about the "welfare state," but the last thing we would think of doing would be to accept responsibility for the public welfare in our personal capacities as Jane Addams did. We rage against the risk of idiotic war in a time in which war means suicide and worse. We repeat, until it is worn of meaning, the old adage about war being too serious a business to be left to the generals. But when it comes to actualities we leave war to the generals as it was never left to them before—and even go as far as to silence each other's protests by agreeing that in military matters criticism may be treason.

When a citizen in our time decides to intervene on his own behalf in the affairs of the world he does not buy a house in the heart of his problem and go live in it himself. He establishes a foundation and staffs it, not with ardent and ignorant amateurs, but with competent professionals directed by a board of experienced advisers. The result, as we all have reason to know, is far more intelligent and efficient public service or social service or educational service than Jane Addams's generation would have thought possible. But the result, for the same reason, is *not* Hull House. Jane Addams was not engaged in social service in this sense. She was not working *for* her immigrants and her poor: she was committing herself *with* them to the common life—that life our generation watches more and more as spectators, as though it were not common, as though it were a life for someone else. She was as explicit about that as a woman could be. She was not, she said, a reformer: she wanted to establish a place "in and around which a fuller life might grow for others *and for herself*." And having made that much clear she then reversed her words to make her declaration clearer still. "The good we secure for ourselves is precarious and uncertain until it is secured for all of us and incorporated into *our common life.*"

No, Hull House changed Chicago and changed the United States, not because it was a successful institution but because it was an eloquent action by a woman capable of action regardless of the dark ahead. We talk as though the great question before our society was whether the things that need to be done in America to keep this last best hope of earth alive should be done by the federal government or by the states or perhaps by the cities or by industries or by some other kind of organization. But that, of course, is not the question. The question before our society is simply whether or not those things *will* be *done.* And the answer is that they will be done if we ourselves see to it as Jane Addams and her friends saw it—if we accept, as she accepted, responsibility for our lives. That, when all is said and done, is why our time remembers her—that she accepted for herself responsibility for the "common life."[1]

In 1965 the concept of Hull House was institutionalized through the Economic Opportunity Act with the establishment of over 900 Community Action Agencies (CAAs); an indispensable step forward in the delivery of social services to our nation's poor. These multi-service agencies have provided basic life-support services to millions of Americans. At present, the Administration is seeking to undo all the positive accomplishments that have been achieved in the past 15 years by these agencies. What is it replacing them with? Vague rhetoric about the "truly needy" and unspecified notions as to *who else might* do the job. Thus, once again, the stark reality is that "The question before our society is simply whether or not those things *will* be *done.*"

We hope that, after reading this *Report*, Americans will come to the conclusion that as a nation we cannot afford to renege on a commitment that is both symbolic and real. To do so would put an inordinate burden on the more than 25 million poor Americans who are already suffering from inflation, unemployment and inadequate social support services. The dire consequences of our nation's inability to put forth and sustain policies and programs are, for the poor, unthinkable, and for our policy-makers, unknowable.

Although it is a rather grim judgment, this Council believes that the resultant despair, hopelessness and lack of opportunity could very well shatter the social equilibrium of our nation. We do not believe that the vast majority of Americans want our government to revert to passivity in the face of critical problems that are national in scope. We believe instead that most Americans want our government to fulfill its responsibility of providing moral leadership that is consistent with the promise of a just and humane society.

---

[1]Reprinted from *A Continuing Journey* by Archibald MacLeish, published by Houghton Mifflin Company, Boston. Copyright ©1967 by Archibald MacLeish. Used by permission.

INTRODUCTION

As the Council was preparing this draft of the *Thirteenth Report*, a battle over the 1982 budget was being fought in Congress. The issue was how much to *cut* social programs and how much to *increase* military spending. During the budget fight, numerous experts in the fields of health care, housing, education, nutrition, energy and employment pointed out how the poor would be forced to sustain an inordinate burden of these cuts. In addition, representatives of nationally recognized organizations representing the poor, the elderly, women, minorities and youth have warned of the serious consequences of these cuts for their constituencies. The language used was very plain and blunt, and ran from "idiotic" to "suicidal."

That Council is fully aware that it is not charged with the responsibility for advising the President and the Congress on either military strategy or overall economic policy. But we are convinced that the connection between national priorities and the terrible potential for human suffering—as well as the bitterness over economic grievances in low-income communities—is real, direct and not an isolated phenomenon. And we cannot remain silent. Particularly when we believe that the social stability of our nation is at stake.

We do have the responsibility to tell our government what we believe to be the truth about poverty in America: that unless this nation changes the direction in which it is heading, unless it makes a new commitment to invest public and private resources in jobs and incomes and housing and health care for the millions of poor and unemployed Americans crowded into the cities and isolated in decaying rural areas, then there is little hope for alleviating the condition of poverty in America. And if that effort is lost, there is no level of defense spending that can make us a secure nation.

This *Report* details how the backing away from antipoverty efforts that pervades the present political discussion will result in a substantial increase in the number of poor, as those who hover just above the poverty level will sink into utter hopelessness. The results are predictable—more crime, physical and psychological illness, broken families, racial division and the potential for violence.

The Council condemns violence in all of its forms, and does not believe that it is ever justified—even as a solution to economic injustice. But we must point out that in a country as rich as America, the continued condition of poverty, while less dramatic than an attack on the streets, is also an act of violence.

In our political and economic system, our nation's most critical social problems often are overshadowed by the crisis of the moment. The Council

1

is concerned that the focus of attention on planning to solve pervasive and critical social, human and "people" problems seems to fade into the background each time we react to a new temporary emergency. These emergencies can take varied forms and often result in different reactions, such as an international crisis—which results in demands for increased military spending; or a domestic "crisis" such as the passage of California's Proposition 13—which spurs demands for cuts in spending for social programs.

These crises distract national attention from poverty, unemployment, poor housing, inadequate health care, decaying urban centers, a faltering education system, unfair tax structures and other social and economic ills of our society. Currently, as a direct result of the first of these crises—in El Salvador and Poland this year, in Iran and Afghanistan last year—the country's spending priorities turn toward increased military hardware, while the plight of millions who lack social and economic opportunity recedes into the background.

One syndicated columnist, citing this syndrome, wrote:

> It's happy times again in the defense industry. There's nothing like an international crisis—Iran, Afghanistan, what-have-you—to overcome, not to say crush, opposition to spending on weaponry.
>
> The Value Line Investment Survey, which serves people trying to make a buck in the stock market, reports: "Increased defense spending is on the way. . . . Most aerospace companies should do well despite the recession." *Business Week*, which serves people trying to get ahead in the business world, reports: "Congress goes wild on defense spending."[2]

We assert that there is another deep, unreported, unheralded crisis going on in America today. It is the crisis in the desperate lives of 55 million poor and near-poor citizens who go to bed each night not knowing whether they will have a job tomorrow, be able to pay the rent or the doctor's bill, or feed the kids. There seem to be no "happy times" ahead for these people.

The Council believes that our nation's defense must and should be a top priority. But we are also troubled with a process of policy discussion in which the choice between alternatives is distorted by the public relations and lobbying practices of the Pentagon and many industries and corporations which are dependent upon defense contracts. The poor are unevenly matched in the adversary politics of the Federal budget. They have few advocates and those they have are without the influence that money and power bring, particularly in the mass media. For example, waste in CETA and other social service programs, even when minimal, has been the butt of much public criticism and facile journalism. Yet waste in military spending, even when well documented, seems to be far more acceptable and less reportable.

The annual budget fight in Congress is largely determined by public opinion polls, which have in turn been influenced by the news media's selection

---

[2]Milton Moskowitz, "Money Tree," *San Francisco Chronicle, April 25, 1980.*

and presentation of events and by the intensive lobbying of powerful special interest groups. Thus, the Council is concerned that critical public policy issues are being affected by private pressures that are not always consistent with our overall national purpose and national priorities.

It has also become fashionable to promote the notion that Federal spending for social programs is inflationary. This Council is on record as having concluded that public spending is not a major cause of inflation. But even if it were, military spending would be *no less* inflationary than civilian public spending, for military spending creates far fewer jobs per dollar spent. One recent study that contrasted military spending with spending on domestic social and economic needs found that the latter creates at least 10,000 more jobs per billion dollars spent. Thus, it would appear that every additional billion dollars deployed for the military deprives the economy of thousands of jobs and deprives millions of people in need of important goods and services. This issue becomes especially important when we consider that the increase for military spending for the next fiscal year is the largest single peacetime military expenditure in our history. And it is projected that the defense budget will double over the next four years.

In the course of researching how the issue of guns-or-butter is treated by the media—and offered to the public—it became quite obvious that both television and print news often, and uncritically, rely on press releases from the Defense Department, the Pentagon and defense industries for their stories.

Yet there are exceptions to the rule. One business and financial reporter for *The New York Times* provided some cogent and thoughtful insights into this very issue in an article for the Business and Finance Section. The article, "Guns Over Butter Equals Inflation," stated:

> Virtually all economists agree, for example, that military spending tends to be inflationary. This is because it puts money into the hands of workers without expanding the supply of goods they can buy—the consumer market for missiles and the like being somewhat limited—thereby driving up the prices of goods like autos and refrigerators and machine tools . . . .
>
> Less widely recognized is the fact that spending on weapons generally produces fewer jobs than many other kinds of Government expenditure. During the economic slowdown in the 1970's, politicians scrambled to lure defense contracts into their districts, despite evidence that a number of public spending alternatives, including many of the kinds of social programs the Administration has decided to curb, would produce more work.
>
> An analysis by Chase Econometrics Associates, examining the potential economic impact of the B-1 bomber, found that both a tax cut and a housing program of equivalent amounts would create more national employment over a 10-year period than would production of the plane. . . . Defense expenditures are concentrated in capital-intensive industries, with relatively few jobs created per

unit of output, while social expenditures benefit such labor-intensive industries as construction, wholesale and retail trade, financial services and the medical and teaching professions.[3]

In reviewing the 1981 budget, other analysts have pointed out that the $1.5 billion research and development budget requested by the Pentagon for the MX missile program is more than the combined research and development budgets for the Department of Labor, the Department of Education, the Community Services Administration, the Department of Transportation, the Environmental Protection Agency, the Federal Drug Administration and the Center for Disease Control.[4]

In the immediate future—as well as in the long run—our national priorities must take into account the millions of Americans who, through no fault of their own, cannot find jobs and who are in desperate need of basic social services. Attempts to balance the budget—at the expense of social programs—and efforts to deliberately shift the economy into a recession—with its concomitant hardships for those who are least able to withstand its effects—will not only fail to make significant inroads towards reducing inflation, but will aggravate our economic problems as well. Moreover, they may also make it even more difficult to balance the budget if the result is sharply increased unemployment. It is estimated that each one percent increase in unemployment will cost the Federal Government, and the nation as a whole, approximately $29 billion as a combination of lost revenue and increased transfer payments. Thus, such policies may bring the budget *more* rather than *less* out of balance.

The Council realizes that there are no easy solutions; but it is clear that a reordering of priorities in favor of human service programs, rather than more military weapons, can benefit the nation as a whole as well as the poor. In focusing attention on our priorities, the Council is reminded of the farewell addresses of both Presidents George Washington and Dwight D. Eisenhower. Washington, who was concerned with domestic responsibilities, in his famous farewell letter cautioned against obsessive hostility toward foreign nations that could lead our nation "astray from its duty and its interest." And President Eisenhower, in a very thoughtful and vigorous statement, warned us against the power and excesses of the "military-industrial complex," and pointed out the real and potential dangers of our larger national interests.

Such a reordering of priorities will not be easy. The economic and political system is filled with powerful special interests who prefer our priorities just as they are. Moreover, those who stand to benefit from, and who most stridently favor higher defense budgets, have a fearsome advantage in presenting their case. It is like the match between David and Goliath. And all too

---

[3]Ann Crittenden, "Guns Over Butter Equals Inflation," *The New York Times*, November 19, 1978, 3(Business and Finance), at 1F.

[4]Moskowitz, *op. cit.*, and Special Analyses, Budget of the United States Government, Fiscal Year 1981, pp. 303–333.

often their case is masked behind technical jargon that—whether by intent or not—tends to confuse the American public, while at the same time they employ jingoism designed to silence opposition by inducing guilt and passivity.

But the task must be undertaken. Issues must be confronted and new ideas introduced, even at the risk of making some of our fellow citizens uncomfortable or embarrassed. Last year the Council attempted to break new ground by asking the question, "What are the conditions needed to create a political climate which would, in fact, help reorder our national priorities so that they are directed toward compassion and more equality and more dignity for all Americans?" And we suggested that the answer might be found by expanding the basic ideal of our nation—more democracy. A year later the meaning is even more relevant. We therefore have repeated and strengthened it.

But time is getting short. And the burned-out neighborhoods in Miami—like Detroit, Watts and Cleveland from earlier years—may well foreshadow the awful possibilities that lie before us if we continue to make the dignity of human life a secondary public concern. In this regard we recall the words of Dr. Martin Luther King, Jr., who, while organizing the "Poor People's March" stated, "Only a tragic death wish can prevent our nation from reordering its priorities."

WOMEN IN POVERTY

Two out of three poor adults are women.[5] Moreover, families headed by women are experiencing a steady decline in their economic status. Why are we experiencing this "feminization of poverty"?[6] What is the role of social welfare programs and policies, and what could be the impact of policy on the poverty faced by women? These questions will be addressed in a discussion focusing on the following themes:

- The decade of the seventies was characterized by a double trend: More of the poor were women, and more women, especially those heading families with minor children, became poor.

- The unusual amount of stress poor women experience exacts a toll on their physical and emotional health. Informal support systems are important, yet they cannot replace a lack of tangible resources. Adequate income is essential for improved well-being.

- The causes of women's poverty are different from those of men's poverty. For example, after a divorce, mothers must often bear the economic as well as emotional responsibility of child-rearing, a burden that often impoverishes the family. U.S. welfare policies do not work for women because they have been based on the "male pauper" model of poverty and do not take account of the special nature of women's poverty.

- Social welfare efforts to reduce welfare dependency and poverty among women are blunted by societal ambivalence toward economic and social independence of women, as well as concerns about maintaining marital stability.

- Inappropriate theories of the causes of poverty and inconsistent policies and goals designed to alleviate it have led to the development of a dual welfare system, divided according to gender and race.

    This process combines with the dual labor market to reinforce economic inequality. Those in the secondary sphere of the labor market, who are increasingly and disproportionately women and minorities, find themselves locked into a combination of welfare and marginal work that can be best characterized as a "workhouse without walls."[7]

---

[5] *A Statistical Portrait of Women in the U.S.,* in *Current Population Reports, Special Study,* (Washington, D.C.: U.S. Department of Commerce, Bureau of the Census). Series P-23, no. 56, 1976.

[6] Diana Pearce, "The Feminization of Poverty: Women, Work and Welfare," *Urban and Social Change Review,* Feb. 1978.

[7] *Ibid.,* p. 35.

- To alleviate women's poverty, social welfare policy must focus on two crucial areas: (1) the services, particularly quality day care, that are essential for wage-earning mothers; and (2) the structures and practices that bar women from jobs now held by men with similar education, skills and experience in the labor force.[8]

American society can reverse the trend toward increased impoverishment of women only by building a social welfare policy that takes into account the distinct nature of women's poverty.

The Feminization of Poverty

Although the number of poor families changed little between 1969 and 1978, its composition shifted dramatically. The number of families with male heads (a group that includes families with a husband and wife as well as male-only families) dropped from 3.2 to 2.6 million, while the number headed by poor women with minor children increased by one-third, from 1.8 to 2.7 million. Today more than half of the total number of poor families are maintained by women.[9]

The seventies saw an even greater shift among black families, as the decrease in poor households headed by black males—from 630,000 to 410,000— was far exceeded by the increase in poor families headed by black females, from 740,000 to 1.2 million. Among families of Spanish origin, about 12 percent of the male-headed and over 50 percent of the female-headed families were poor (see Table 1).[10]

Families with female heads have a poverty rate six times that of male-headed families (31.4 percent vs. 5.3 percent; see Table 1). When race is taken into account, the poverty rate also increases so that minority families supported by women have even higher rates. More than half of the families with female heads live in poverty, and 40 percent of all black children are poor.

The most recently reported median income for white families nationwide was $18,370; for Hispanic families, $12,570; and for black families, $10,880.[11] The median income of single mothers was much lower than that

---

[8]Providing essential support services, particularly day care, for women in the paid labor force may enlarge the pool of jobs. But breaking down artificial barriers of gender, as well as race, may simply alter the composition of the poor. That is, if poverty were "de-sexed" and racially integrated, it might then become apparent that unemployment and poverty are structural problems, and not ones associated with particular groups or individuals (e.g., that there are simply not enough jobs to go around). But the current trend is just the opposite, towards a concentration of poverty among women and minorities. The structure of the American economy may well have taken a very different form by the time poverty is distributed equally between men and women, and between whites and minorities.

[9]*Characteristics of the Population Below the Poverty Level: 1978*, in *Current Population Reports*, (Washington, D.C.: U.S. Department of Commerce, Bureau of the Census). Series P–60, No. 124, July 1980.

[10]*Ibid.*

[11]*The Status of Children, Youth and Families, 1979*, (Washington, D.C.: Department of Health and Human Services, Administration of Children, Youth and Families) 1980.

TABLE 1
Percentage of Families in Poverty in 1978, By Sex, Race and Age of Head, and Presence of Children[1]

	All Families	Families with Male Head	Families with Female Head
All Families	9.1%	5.3%	31.4%
White Families	6.9	4.7	23.5
Head < 25 years old	13.2	6.4	53.6
With related children < 18 years old	9.3	4.7	33.5
Black Families	27.5	11.8	50.6
Head < 25 years old	49.0	20.4	69.5
With related children < 18 years old	34.4	11.8	58.8
Families of Spanish Origin	20.0	12.4	53.1
Head < 25 years old	30.6		
With related children < 18 years old	24.1		[2]68.9

Source: *Characteristics of the Population Below the Poverty Level: 1978,* (Washington, D.C.: U.S. Department of Commerce, Bureau of the Census). Series P-60, No. 124, 1980.

[1]Poverty status is defined as having a money income below the poverty threshold, which is approximately three times the cost of an "emergency" minimal diet, varied by farm/nonfarm status and size of family. (See *Characteristics, Ibid.,* for further details.) For a nonfarm family of four in 1978, the figure was $6662.

[2]Figure is for persons, rather than families (the latter was not given), and is probably several points higher than the family figure would be.

of two-parent families. White mothers had a median income that was only 38 percent of the median income of two-parent white families; similarly, the income of Hispanic mothers was 38 percent of average Hispanic family income; and the income of black mothers was 40 percent of black family income.[12]

Some of the trends within groups shown by Table 1 may appear to be contradictory. For example, though income of individual blacks has increased, black family income has *decreased* in relation to that of non-blacks.[13] This is because the number of black families with multiple earners is decreasing, and a rising proportion of black families are headed by women.

The number of black families with multiple earners fell by 15 percent,

[12]*Ibid.*

[13]Reynolds Farley, "Trends in Racial Inequalities: Have the Gains of the 1960's Disappeared in the 1970's?", *American Sociological Review,* Vol. 42, No. 2, 1977.

while that of Hispanic families increased by 4 percent, and that of white families increased by 13 percent. At the same time white families with only one earner declined by 25 percent.[14] The largest change, however, is in the category of families with no earners. While the proportions of Hispanic and white families without an adult earner increased by 29 percent and 34 percent, respectively, the proportion of black families in this category increased by 50 percent during the decade of the seventies.[15] There has been a marked decline in the proportion of poor families in all groups. The recent recession and the present economic uncertainty have forced many more families into poverty.

Ways in Which Women are Disadvantaged in the Labor Market. If wives and female heads of households were paid the wages that similarly qualified men earn, about half of the families now living in poverty would not be poor.[16] These women workers are handicapped by higher unemployment and discouraged worker rates, more involuntary part-time and seasonal work, fewer increases in income over one's lifetime, and an earnings gap (between male and female) that is widening.

The unemployment rates of women are only slightly higher than those of men. However, unemployment rates are misleading for they count only those who are consistently looking for employment. Those who wisk to work but are not actively seeking work are termed "discouraged workers." Millions of Hispanics, blacks and women have given up and entered the underclass permanently.

Many believe the incomes of women workers are low because they choose part-time or seasonal work. Yet of those women who headed households and worked fewer than 50 weeks in the previous year, one-third stated that they did so because they were unable to find work.[17]

An important addition to the incomes of many workers is the lucrative overtime work. While approximately one-quarter of men workers work overtime, half that number of women workers do, with comparable effects on income.[18]

Women workers are also at a disadvantage in terms of union membership. One study calculated the value of union membership in the mid-seventies as an increment of approximately $650 in annual income.[19] The proportion of

[14] *The Status of Children, Youth and Families, 1979, op. cit.*

[15] *Ibid.*

[16] Patricia C. Sexton, *Women and Work* (R & D Monograph No. 46), (Washington, D.C.: U.S. Department of Labor, Employment and Training Administration) 1977.

[17] *Characteristics of the Population Below the Poverty Level: 1978, op. cit.*

[18] *The Earning Gap Between Women and Men*, (Washington, D.C.: U.S. Department of Labor, Women's Bureau) 1979.

[19] Sally Hillsman Baker, "Women in Blue-Collar and Service Occupations," in A. Stromger and B. Harkess, eds., *Women Working*, (Palo Alto, California: Mayfield Publishing Co.) 1977.

women workers who are union members has been declining since 1950, from approximately 15 percent to 11 percent in the late seventies.[20] Also important, particularly for women who provide the major earnings of their households, are the fringe benefits of union membership, including health benefits and supplementary unemployment payments.

The 2,380,000 women who are year-round, full-time workers account for approximately one-third of the paid labor force, but they account for 53 percent of those who earn less than $5000 per year. (Figures are for 1977, at which time an annual salary at the minimum wage was about $4800.) In contrast, of full-time, year-round workers who earn $15,000 or more, only 9 percent are women.[21] One effect of these handicaps and low earnings is that the presence of earners in households headed by women does not necessarily eliminate poverty. In fact, 21 percent of female-headed households with income from earnings are *still* poor.[22] More than one-third of single mothers with children under six who work full-time at paid labor are poor.[23]

Adolescent Women.   Gender and minority status constitute especially acute problems for teenagers. Teenage mothers enjoy little economic mobility; many never earn more than they did at age 16, while the earning curves for men continue to rise during their early and middle years.[24] Young adults born in the "baby boom" after World War II have been confronted with overcrowded schools and a depressed economy. Demographers see this group of children as having a profound impact on our society. Their sheer numbers have trapped them into a permanent disadvantaged status. They caused overcrowding in schools and colleges throughout the U.S., resulting in massive building programs for schools that now stand empty.

These young people then entered a shrinking labor market, and their rate of entry into the job market was six times that of the previous generation. The negative impact of this baby boom generation was temporarily delayed when many of its members were sent to college and thousands were sent to Vietnam. But now, young adults, even members of the traditionally privileged class, face a bleak future. The minority teenager has become a permanent member of the underclass whose prospects are worse now than they were for any group during the Great Depression.[25]

---

[20]Linda H. LeGrande, "Women in Labor Organizations: Their Ranks are Increasing," *Monthly Labor Review*, August 1978.

[21]*The Earning Gap, op. cit.*

[22]*Characteristics of the Population Below the Poverty Level: 1978, op. cit.*

[23]*Families Maintained by Female Households 1970-1979* in *Current Population Reports*, (Washington, D.C.: U.S. Department of Commerce, Bureau of the Census). Series P-23, No. 101. The Council points out that if the costs of child day-care were taken into account in determining income status, there would be a significant increase in the number of full-time employed single mothers classified as poor.

[24]U.S. Civil Rights Commission, quoted in *Washington Post*, August 2, 1980, p. A2.

[25]L. Jones, *America and the Baby Boom Generation*, (New York: Coward Books) 1980.

Transitions in Family Structure. The dissolution rate of marriages is almost exactly what it was a century ago, about 34.5 per 1000 marriages per year. But the major cause of dissolution has changed. A century ago divorce accounted for only 3.5 percent of all marriages that were ended. Today it accounts for 44 percent of dissolutions. Even as late as 1951, more than half of the female-headed households were headed by widows. Today widows head less than one-third of such households.

While many of today's widows are older than those of a century ago, more women who head households now are young mothers with young children to support. Between 1960 and 1978, the percentage of female-headed households with children younger than 18 increased from 57 percent to 69 percent of all female-headed households. Among minority female-headed households the percentage with children is 81 percent.[26]

Not only will fewer female-headed households be headed by widows, but more families will be experiencing marital disruption due to divorce, which has doubled since 1963. Two out of every five marriages in the United States end in divorce, and the figures are higher for teenage marriages. The most recent data indicate that 50 percent of all children can expect to live in one-parent homes for a significant part of their lives.[27]

The proportion of white families headed by women increased from 8 to 12 percent between 1970 and 1978; and black female-headed families increased from 31 to 37 percent.[28] However, there is a racial difference in the meaning of this status. Single white women tend to marry, or marry a second time. Black women, however, tend to remain single, in part because of the excess of black females compared to males at the ages when most people marry.

The number of single parents who were never married has soared 109 percent chiefly because of teenage pregnancy. Single parents whose spouses were absent (because of military service, job responsibilities, illness or jail) increased by 24 percent, and those who were separated increased by 29 percent. The number of widows increased by 15 percent.[29]

Financial Supports in Female-Headed Families. Ironically, as the proportion of female family heads who are widows has decreased, the financial and social security of widows has increased. Table 2 indicates the wide variation in the incidence of poverty by marital status, which reflects class differences (desertion is often the ''divorce'' of the poor) and the different sources of support each marital status group receives.

The typical outcome of a marital breakup in a family with children is that the man becomes *single*, while the woman becomes a *single parent*. Unlike

---

[26]*Characteristics of the Population, op. cit.*

[27]*The Status of Children, Youth and Families, 1979, op. cit.*

[28]Beverly L. Johnson, ''Women Who Head Families, 1970–1977: Their Number Rose, Income Lagged,'' *Monthly Labor Review,* February 1978; and *Characteristics of the Population, op. cit.*

[29]*The Status of Children, Youth and Families, 1978, op. cit.*

TABLE 2
1978 Poverty Rates of Female-Headed
Families, by Marital Status

Marital Status of Household Head	Percent in Poverty (1978)
Widowed	15.1%
Divorced	26.1
Single (never married)	46.2
Married, husband absent	50.5

Source: *Characteristics of the Population Below the Poverty Level: 1978,* (Washington, D.C.: U.S. Department of Commerce, Bureau of the Census). Series P-60, No. 124, 1980.

widows whose economic loss has been made less devastating by Social Security, including Supplemental Security Income (SSI) and Old Age Survivor Disability Insurance (OASDI), other groups of single parents rarely find private and public transfers sufficient to make up the deficit.

A national survey in 1975 found that only 25 percent of those eligible actually received child support, and that 60 percent of those who did received less than $1500.[30] These awards tend to be low, in part because they are based on the needs of two-parent families with no child day-care costs, and in part because judges permit the absent parent to deduct the cost of maintaining his household—including the costs of time payments on cars, recreation and entertainment—from what he would pay as child support. The result is that half the fathers who did pay support were contributing less than 10 percent of their income.

In the group of single families that result from divorce, black women fared worst in terms of child-support payments. Child-support payments were awarded by the court to 71 percent of the white women, 44 percent of the Hispanic women, and only 29 percent of the black women. The level of support payments showed the same pattern: The white mother was awarded $2800; the Hispanic mother, $1320; and the black mother, $1290.

Poorly educated women are less likely to receive alimony, child support or maintenance payments.[31] Less than half of the 12 million divorced women received property following divorce, but in 1979 the median value of property received was only $4650.[32]

---

[30]Joanne Schulman, "Poor Women and Family Law," *Clearinghouse Review*, February 1981.

[31]Child Support and Alimony, *Special Study,* (Washington, D.C.: U.S. Department of Commerce, Bureau of the Census). Series P-23, No. 106, 1978.

[32]"Divorced Women: The Myth of Alimony, Property Settlements and Child Support," *Marriage and Divorce Today*, November 24, 1980.

For the 1.4 million mothers who have never been married, the situation is extremely bleak. Only 8 percent were slated to receive support, and only 5 percent ever received any payments.[33]

For women who rely on public transfer payments, the picture is equally dismal. Depending on the state, welfare payments range from 49 to 96 percent of the poverty level.[34] The average family payment in 1977 was $241 per month. (The average size of a family on welfare is approximately three persons.)[35] The real value of the average welfare payment, accounting for inflation and the declining size of recipient households, has decreased by approximately 20 percent in the last decade.[36] Table 3 shows payment levels of some states. Female-headed families that were maintained on non-employed income averaged $5314 in 1978, while all female-headed families averaged $10,689.

These amounts stand in stark contrast to the average income for families headed by men (including husband-wife families), which was $21,703.[37] While death halts the "private transfer," or sharing of income from husband to wife, divorce or desertion has virtually the same effect on a woman's economic status. The woman whose former partner is still alive is likely to be more devastated economically than a widow, whose plight is addressed through Social Security and other assistance programs.

Aid to Families with Dependent Children (AFDC) originally grew out of concern about the damage the loss of a father would be to the family, yet today there is virtually no sanction, either legal or informal, against the father who contributes little or nothing for the support of his offspring. Nor, where fathers cannot or will not pay, is the attempt to ameliorate the poverty of the mothers and children even minimally adequate.

Stress, Poverty and the Single Mother

The most vulnerable aspect of the female-headed home is finances. All families of all races experienced a loss of real income between 1973 and 1978.[38] The lower income of black families, and specifically black female-headed families, placed many at or below the poverty level (Table 1). To meet even the most minimal developmental needs of children and mothers, the family support system must be augmented by external resources. Since not all single mothers function with a kin-help network, their support needs must be augmented by community-based programs.

---

[33]*Ibid.*

[34]Sar A. Levitan, *Programs in Aid of the Poor for the 1980's,* Fourth Edition, (Baltimore: Johns Hopkins Press) 1980.

[35]Dorothy T. Lang, "Poor Women and Health Care," *Clearinghouse Review,* February 1981.

[36]Unpublished memorandum.

[37]*Characteristics of the Population, op. cit.*

[38]*The Status of Children, Youth and Families,* 1979.

TABLE 3
Average Monthly AFDC Payments Per Person
June 1979

State	Average Payment
Mississippi	$26
Alabama	38
Texas	36
Illinois	84
Indiana	65
District of Columbia	83
New York	119
Maine	77
North Dakota	92
Arizona	92
California	53
Washington	115
Virginia	74

Source: Sar Levitan, *Programs in Aid of the Poor for the 1980's,* (Baltimore: The John Hopkins Press) 1980, p. 31.

Research has shown that single-parent mothers experience a level of stress significantly higher than that experienced by other groups. Within the single-parent mother population, those who have never been married experience even greater strain. Their children, often the result of out-of-wedlock teenage pregnancies, are born into the most precarious mother-child units in our society. Several authors have detailed the unfavorable physical, emotional and social impact of teenage pregnancy.[39]

The ecology of the black family predisposes it to continuous stress, in addition to the normal developmental strains experienced by all families. Despite the cultural preference for meeting crises and family needs within the extended kin-help network and then through friends, families may often experience a level of stress and lowered personal satisfaction that forces them to seek assistance from the wider community.

Even when they were well above the poverty level, single mothers in one study experienced significantly more tension than those who were married.[40]

The stress experienced by low-income mothers is occasioned by crises as

[39]W. Hambridge, "Teen Clinics," *Obstetrics and Gynecology,* Vol. 43, No. 3, 1974; M. Lane, "Contraception for Adolescents," *Family Planning Perspectives,* Vol. 5, No. 1, Winter 1973; and J. Dravits and S. Smith, "The Acceptance of a Family Clinic by Recently Delivered Teenagers," *Southern Medical Journal,* Vol. 67, No. 7, July 1974.

[40]H. McAdoo, "Factors Related to Stability in Upwardly Mobile Black Families," *Journal of Marriage and the Family,* Vol. 40, No. 4, 1978.

well as ongoing conditions. On a checklist of 91 life events requiring change and readjustment, most community surveys have shown that individuals experience an average of two such events a year.[41] In contrast, mothers in a Boston study of 43 black and white low-income women reported an average of 14 such events during the past two years.[42] Though their lives included violent and emotionally exhausting events, the lack of money took greatest toll on their mental health. Depression levels were high in these women living in high-density, high-crime urban areas.

A later study showed that working-class single mothers who were employed but still earned salaries that placed them just above the poverty level, were under extreme stress caused by finances, housing concerns and problems at work, in that order.[43] Many felt they were underpaid but wanted to work because, as one women stated, she had once been on welfare and that was "the worst experience in my life." Safe, dependable child day-care was needed. Mothers tended to be particularly bothered by the conflicting demands of motherhood, employment and their social and private lives.

Extended Family Help Patterns. One of the strongest black and ethnic-minority cultural patterns is extensive help systems. The family's effective environment is composed of a network of relatives, friends and neighbors that provides emotional support and economic supplements and, most important, protects the family's integrity from assault by external forces.

Viewing the higher proportion of one-parent families as unstable ignores the extended family adaptation bonds.[44] Many groups maintain a strong extended family system despite mobility.[45] Only recently have researchers begun to recognize similar patterns in black families. Functionality of the home is positively related to the parent's ability to manipulate the American economic system. The black extended family has demonstrated that it is a source of strength and a protection against isolation in the larger society.[46]

The degree of kin interaction is often overlooked in research studies that focus only on structural features. There is a need to determine the norms and values of family interaction and to examine how the process relates to the forces shaping it.[47] The kinship network is more than an extension of family

[41]B. Dohrenwend, "Social Status and Stressful Life Events," *Journal of Personality and Social Psychology,* Vol. 28, 1973, pp. 225-235.

[42]B. Bell, *et al.*, "Depression and Low-Income Female-Headed Families," *Families Today,* Vol. 1, NIMG Science Monograph, (Rockville, Md.: U.S. Department of Health and Human Services) 1979.

[43]H. McAdoo, "Role of Black Women in Maintaining Stability and Mobility in Black Families," L. Rose (Ed.), *The Black Woman: Current Research and Theory,* (Beverly Hills, California: Sage Publications) May 1980.

[44]C. Hamilton, "Just How Unstable is the Black Family?" *The New York Times,* August 1, 1971.

[45]M. Sussman, *Sourcebook in Marriage and the Family,* (Boston: Houghton Mifflin) 1974.

[46]R. Hill, *The Strengths of Black Families,* (New York: Emerson Hall) 1971.

[47]R. Staples, *The Black Women in America,* (Chicago: Nelson Hall Publishing) 1973.

relationships.[48] It can be considered a system of social relationships derived from birth and marriage and pertaining to an individual's place in society. The major activity of the kin network is the exchange of material and non-material help. Friends and relatives often support the mother's activities outside the home, but they may not attempt to intervene as a family member might do. They also care for the children when the mother must be alone or when she attempts to establish a social life.

The use of social networks has been shown to be important to the functioning of successful single parents.[49] In one study, the support system and proven coping patterns of single Puerto Rican mothers were found to be most important to maintaining their stability. Their support structures were composed of their relatives (usually their mothers and sisters), boyfriends or former husbands, neighbors and religious beliefs. Ability to control their own fertility and the ability to participate in community affairs and advanced education were most helpful.

Of course, inherent in any support is a degree of reciprocity. These informal supports are often the only means of survival for a working mother. Not all mothers live near relatives or desire to be totally dependent upon kin. The ties they form with other mothers and close friends increase their ability to cope with the stress of their multiple roles.

Many tactics are used to increase the number of individuals who share in the reciprocal obligations. Enlarging the circle of persons who may be called upon in cases of need beyond the household increases the security of the individual. The "friend network" can be considered a kind of community, a social world outside of the single parent's home.[50]

While often emotionally supportive, the extended family can provide only limited financial help to a poor family in poverty, for kin networks are not responsible for creating or alleviating poverty itself.

Causes and Cures for Poverty: Men vs. Women

Women are poor for different reasons than men are poor. This is not to say that needy women and men do not ever share poverty-causing characteristics; in fact, many women are poor because their husbands are poor. But, increasingly, many women are poor "in their own right," and yet know very little about female poverty.

One way to understand the distinctive nature of poverty among women is to study the various factors and causes of poverty by gender. In Table 4 these

---

[48]E. Farber, *Kinship and Class*, (New York: Basic Books) 1971.

[49]A. Barry, "A Research Project on Successful Single-Parent Families," *American Journal of Family Therapy*, Vol. 7, No. 3, Fall 1979, pp. 65–73.

[50]R. Weiss, *Going it Alone, the Family Life and Social Situation of the Single Parent*, (New York: Basic Books) 1979.

TABLE 4
Theories of Poverty[1]

Origin	Internal Causes (Locus Within Poor)	Intermediate	External Causes (Locus Outside of Poor in Institutions, Organization and Groups)
Personal	**Physical:** *Physical burdens and complications of childbearing. Higher levels of childbirth, early marriages and/or early childbearing.*	Poor health; part-time employment; disability; poor neonatal health.	*Inadequate prenatal health care; lack of family planning information and minimal access to information.*
	Emotional: Low commitment to work; learned dependency; drugs or alcohol addiction; criminal "tendencies"		Personal racism and *sexism of employers and educators;* awareness of sex/race "job ceiling."
	Educational: Lack of achievement.	Age ("too" young or "too" old).	Outmoded skills; inadequate skills.
Intermediate (Organizations, Groups)	*Lack of socialization to roles of primary responsibility, in either employment or family life.*	Adolescent parenting; single parenting.	*Lack of day care and related services supportive of employment.*
	Lack of child support.	Limited in education; Low birth weight = poorer health = lower school achievement.	*Single parent: imbalance in sex ratio among blacks.*
Social		Part-time, and/or seasonal jobs.	Lack of sex/race role models; inferior schooling.
			Poor preventive health care.

Socialization to appropriate sex and race; lower status occupational roles; socialization to acquire less, and/or sex stereotyped education.

Institutional sexism and discrimination by employers and educators; institutional racism and discriminatory employers and educators; *dual labor market;* lack of enough jobs and appropriate opportunities for all who can work outside the home.

Educational; low motivation to excel.

Occupational segregation.

Characteristics of Specific Labor Market (unemployment rate, etc.); curricula both *sex- and race-typed.*

Source: Chesler, *op. cit.*

¹Those factors which cause poverty for women only are italicized. Most causes are interrelated and mutually reinforcing. For example, lack of birth control information may result in early childbearing and/or single parenting, and the poverty of these mothers may in the future be reinforced by their inability, in a sex-segregated labor market, to obtain sufficient wages to support themselves. The placement of factors is somewhat arbitrary; thus the low education of some who grew up in the South may be entirely institutional in its origin, while low education in the urban North may be the result of individual choice, lack of education opportunities, family poverty, expulsion (e.g., for pregnancy or other reasons), or a combination of such individual, institutional and organizational factors.

factors are schematically arranged, using a modification of a method developed to categorize theories of racial inequality.[51]

The various theories are arranged along two dimensions. The horizontal dimension ranges from causes of poverty originating within the victims themselves at one extreme, to those originating outside the victim group at the other. In the latter case the fault may be found within organizations and institutions. The vertical dimension ranges from individual or psychological in character, to causes that are societal or cultural (including subcultural).

Arraying these various factors along two continua indicates the origins of poverty and the fundamental differences in where theories pinpoint the roots of poverty. The listing of these theories is not meant to imply that all are equally valid as explanations of poverty or equally important as sources of poverty.

Table 4 illustrates how the poverty experienced by women is different from that experienced by men. Each theory or cause that applies to women exclusively or in the overwhelming majority of instances is italicized. With the possible exception of a criminal record, none of the causes of poverty listed here is generically male, while roughly half of those listed are generically female. Thus women, especially minority women, may be poor for some of the same reasons as men, but few men become poor because of "female" causes.

Men generally do not become poor because of divorce, sex-role socialization, sexism or, of course, pregnancy. Indeed, some may lift themselves out of poverty by the same means that plunge women into it: The same divorce that frees a man from the financial burdens of a family may result in poverty for his ex-wife and children.

Distinct reasons for the poverty among women can be traced back to two sources. First, in American culture *women continue to carry the major burden of childrearing.* This sex-role socialization has many ramifications. For example, women tend to make career choices that anticipate that they will interrupt their participation in the labor force to bear children, and a woman is the parent who wins child custody in the overwhelming majority of cases.[52] The second major source of poverty among women is the kind of opportunities, or more accurately, the limited opportunities available to women in the labor market. Occupational segregation, sex discrimination and sexual harassment combine to limit both income and mobility for women workers.[53] The interaction of these two sources is illustrated by society's view of child care and child-care workers. Since childrearing is primarily a female responsibility, it is virtually only women who do child-care work, whether in their

---

[51]Mark Chesler, "Contemporary Sociological Theories of Racism," in Phillis A. Katz, ed., *Towards the Elimination of Racism,* (New York: Pergamon Press) 1976.

[52]Allyson S. Grossman, "Divorced and Separated Women in the Labor Force—An Update," *Monthly Labor Review,* October 1978.

[53]M. Blaxall and B. Reagan, *Women and the Workplace: The Implications of Occupational Segregation,* (Chicago: University of Chicago Press) 1976.

homes or in child day-care centers. Since it is women who pay for child day-care, either because they have custody or because it is viewed as an expense incurred because the *wife* is working outside the home, and because so many women earn substantially less than men, child day-care workers earn very low wages.

Thus the two fundamental sources of female poverty combine to keep women in an economic "ghetto." When these factors interact with minority status, youth or old age, there is an even greater likelihood of being poor.

Poverty among men, by contrast, is often seen as the consequence of joblessness, and therefore it is concluded that the cure for poverty is a job. Only the *theories* as to what causes joblessness have varied. When the primary cause was considered alcoholism, then alcohol treatment or efforts to outlaw alcohol were emphasized. When it was thought to be the result of laziness, workhouses and poorhouses were set up. When it was believed to be the result of racial discrimination, equal opportunity programs and affirmative action requirements were instituted. In each case, however, the program's goal was to put the poor to work. It was assumed that once employed, people would no longer be poor.

For most poor men, the "ball game" is overcoming barriers to employment. Most men who work can support themselves and their families. In one study, less than five percent of families with children and a male wage-earner were in poverty.[54]

But many women cannot, by themselves, support themselves and their families. Women who work outside the home full-time, year-round, earn only 59 percent of what men earn.[55] Particularly for those poor women, who are generally lower than average in skills and education, getting a job is not a panacea. Since the woman with a college education earns less on the average than a man with an eighth-grade education, the opportunity for a woman with an eighth-grade education to earn a "living wage" is considerably limited.[56]

Poverty among hundreds of thousands of women already working underlines the failure of the "job" solution. Of the mothers working outside the house who headed households with children less than 18 years old in 1978, more than one-quarter had incomes below the poverty level.[57] Even among those currently on welfare, a substantial portion are also in the labor force (about 24 percent), while of those who are long-term recipients of AFDC, one-half have been employed within the past year.[58] In other words, even a full-time job does not provide a route out of poverty for women with the same certainty that it does for most men who are poor.

---

[54] *Characteristics of the Population Below the Poverty Level: 1978, op. cit.*

[55] *Ibid.*

[56] *The Earnings Gap, op. cit.*

[57] *Characteristics of the Population Below the Poverty Level: 1978, op. cit.*

[58] "Long-term" refers to those who received public assistance for four or more consecutive years out of the last seven; see Martin Rein and Lee Rainwater, "Patterns of Welfare Use," *Social Service Review,* December 1978.

Why does the "job" solution not work for women? First, occupational segregation confines women to job "ghettoes" where the pay is low and the mobility is little or nonexistent. The concentration of women in a handful of jobs is extreme: 60 percent of all women are found in 10 occupations, including nursing and elementary teaching.[59] Almost all of the "new" jobs for women that have emerged, particularly in the seventies, have been in traditionally female-dominated areas such as retail sales, and are occupations that tend to be low-wage and dead end. It is precisely such new "opportunities" that are available to women entering the labor market. The latest data suggest that this concentration and segregation does not seem to be declining.[60]

Second, those women who manage to avoid female job ghettoes encounter sex discrimination in salaries, promotions, benefits and/or sexual harassment. Breaching admissions barriers of previously male-dominated (often, white male-dominated) occupations and professions does not bring immediate and full equal opportunity.

These difficulties are exacerbated if the women involved are minority women. The experience of women who have sought jobs outside of traditionally female occupations parallels that of the small number of black children who attended white schools in the South under "freedom of choice" desegregation plans. In both instances, the newcomers encountered harassment, social isolation, and denigration of their personal integrity and motivation.

Given that a job often does not alleviate poverty for women, nor enable them to leave welfare, what has been the response of the welfare system? In brief, it has been to continue its obsession with the question of work incentives, and to develop programs that deal with barriers to employment often experienced by *men*—lack of job search skills, experience in the labor force or job training—while ignoring the special problems women face, such as segregation, sex discrimination and sexual harassment. In other words, the welfare system continues to push the recipient—who is almost always a woman—to go to work outside the home, even if employment neither lifts her from poverty nor frees her from welfare.

Welfare programs force women into the labor market and reinforce their economic disadvantages in a number of ways.

In the decade of the seventies, several programs, most notably the Work Incentive Program (WIN) were transformed in a way that decreased their effectiveness for women. These changes included de-emphasizing vocational and on-the-job training in favor of direct job placement, particularly in jobs created by the Comprehensive Employment and Training Act (CETA). In addition, some services, particularly child care and transportation, were decreased. It is not surprising, therefore, that although men represented only 26 percent of the WIN registrants, they accounted for over one-third of those

---

[59]Stromger and Harkess.

[60]Francine D. Blau and Wallace E. Hendricks, "Occupational Segregation by Sex. Trends and Prospects," *The Journal of Human Resources*, Vol. 14, No. 2.

who secured unsubsidized jobs. many women who are potentially eligible for the WIN program have been exempted because they have a child under six years old, are needed in the home as a caretaker or are aged, ill or disabled. Child care, of course, is not provided as part of the program itself; likewise, although 90 percent of the women in CETA have children, these programs also fail to provide child care. In short, if they do not fit the "male pauper" model, then they do not fit the program.[61]

CETA programs, although not usually targeted as "welfare" programs, were designed not only to serve women equally, but also to overcome "sex-stereotyping" in occupational assignment. However, inequality and sex-stereotyping were not eliminated in these programs. In one case, a women CETA participant sued her program because she had been offered the choice of secretarial or cooking class. When she sought to transfer to a computer repair class, she was refused. At the same time, a male student in the secre-tarial class was allowed to transfer.[62]

Several evaluations of CETA and WIN have indicated that women, minorities and youth have been under-served, both in comparison to their proportion in the population, and in proportion to their registration in the program.[63] Particularly where the training programs have been in occupa-tions traditionally dominated by males, few women have participated.[64]

Sometimes women and men receive different forms of training. Women receive small stipends or "work experience" at the minimum wage, while men receive public-service jobs which are full time and pay $8000 per year and up.[65]

The structure of CETA and inadequate monitoring procedures of CETA also make it difficult to determine exactly how well women are being served, but it is clear that gender-related differences do occur.

Programs such as WIN and CETA not only provide employment oppor-tunities for disproportionately more men, but they also increase the earnings of men more than of women. In 1978 WIN placed women in jobs whose average entry wage was $2.97 per hour, and less than five percent were paid more than $5.00 per hour. In contrast, the men placed through WIN aver-aged $4.01 per hour, and more than 20 percent entered jobs paying $5.00 per hour or more.[66]

Inconsistencies in social welfare policy may reflect the general am-bivalence in American society about the role and status of women. Enabling

[61]Unpublished memorandum.

[62]Deborah Bachrach, "Women in Employment," *Clearinghouse Review*, February 1981.

[63]Donald C. Baumer, C. Van Horn and M. Marvel, "Explaining Benefit Distribution in CETA Programs," *The Journal of Human Resources*, Vol. 14, No. 2.

[64]"Need to Ensure Non-Discrimination in CETA Programs," (Washington, D.C.: Office of the Comptroller General), June 17, 1980. HRD–80–95(GAO).

[65]Baumer, et al.

[66]B. L. McDonald and R. Diehl, "Women and Welfare", *Clearinghouse Review*, Vol. 14, No. 11, February 1981.

women to become "primary" earners is not yet a societal goal. While it has become increasingly acceptable and even expected that a woman will work outside the home, it is also expected that her job will be secondary both to her husband's job (the husband still being the "primary" earner) and to her home and family responsibilities. The stability of the marriage is often considered to be endangered if the woman earns more than her spouse. Yet more and more women are becoming displaced homemakers and/or heads of their own households. For these women, the social role of "secondary" earner is clearly dysfunctional and almost guarantees poverty.

"Female independence" has two components: social independence, that is, heading one's own household; and economic independence, being economically self-sufficient. As for social independence, policy makers have long worried that welfare programs generally, as well as some welfare policies specifically, may inadvertently cause marriages to break up and/or encourage the formation of single-parent households. For example, the development of the Aid to Families with Dependent Children - Unemployed Parent (AFDC-UP) programs in many states was based on the conviction that eligibility for welfare should not be predicated on the unemployed father leaving the home. Much concern has also been expressed about the finding that the families in the Negative Income Experiment who received high and guaranteed incomes compared to similar families using the regular welfare programs had significantly higher divorce rates than their counterparts.[67]

Certainly, social welfare programs should not cause families to break up, nor should they exacerbate the poverty that women and children frequently experience as a result of such break-ups. But there is strong evidence that the role social welfare programs play in family break-ups is not primary. First, the rate of divorce has been rising steadily but dramatically at all income levels. It would be difficult to argue that middle-class families that break up do so for such reasons as incompatibility and unfaithfulness, but poor families do so in order to become eligible for welfare, especially since many of those receiving AFDC were middle-class families before their marriages ended.[68]

Second, one should at least ask what kind of marriage and family life previously existed in the families, such as those in the Negative Income Experiment, for whom a relatively small increment of guaranteed income apparently allowed families to exercise the option of divorce. There is much evidence, for example, that children who are raised in an unhappy but unbroken home suffer sometimes more ill effects (such as low academic achievement and juvenile delinquency) than do children with similar problems in single-parent homes. This is not to suggest that divorce and/or single parenthood are uniformly positive, but rather that an increase in them is a social

[67]John Bishop, "Jobs, Cash Transfers and Marital Instability: A Review in Synthesis of the Evidence," *The Journal of Human Resources*, Vol. XV, No. 3, Fall 1980.

[68]Nancy R. Mudrick, The Use of AFDC by Previously High- and Low-Income Households," *Social Service Review*, March 1978.

trend upon which social welfare policies can have relatively little impact. In short, this trend should be treated, at least by public agencies, as a given. To treat it otherwise is to develop, *de facto*, two sets of rules, one for the poor and one for the nonpoor. That is, while the nonpoor are permitted to choose freely among life-styles, the poor are presented with the choice of marriage or poverty (at least for the women and children). Contemporary welfare policy may already be forcing such a choice; one of the most often cited reasons for leaving AFDC is marriage.

Social welfare efforts to make the poor women self-supporting have frequently enabled them to enter the labor force as only marginal workers. For increasing numbers of women, the presence of even a few dependent children has required combining employment and welfare, concurrently or alternately.[69]

Dual Welfare Systems, Dual Labor Markets and Gender Inequality

The concept of the dual labor market has been developed elsewhere.[70] This concept divides the labor market into two spheres, the primary and the secondary. Relatively few workers move between the two. The *primary sector* is characterized by high wages, job security, fringe benefits, opportunities for advancement, a high degree of unionization, and due process in terms of job rights. The *secondary sector* is characterized by low wages, low security, part-time and seasonal work, few fringe benefits, little protection from arbitrary employer actions, and a low rate of unionization.

The duality in the welfare system complements and supports the inequality in the labor market itself. Over all, the *primary sector* of welfare seeks to minimize the costs to the individual when the system fails, as when there is high unemployment in a geographically concentrated industry. It seeks to enable workers to move from job to job without impoverishing them or their families.

The *secondary welfare sector*, on the other hand, seeks to provide only the most minimal support necessary to meet basic needs. It also seeks to subsidize low-wage workers (and through them, low-wage industries) by providing some of the support services, such as health care through Medicaid, found in the fringe benefits of the primary sector.[71]

---

[69]Rein and Rainwater, *op. cit.*

[70]David M. Gordon, *Theories of Poverty and Underemployment: Orthodox, Radical and Dual Labor Market Perspectives,* (Lexington, Mass.: Health & Co.) 1972.

[71]There is an incentive for the employer to reinforce this dual welfare/labor market. By hiring mostly women, and paying them low wages and/or firing them in ways so that they use AFDC as unemployment compensation, or as a wage supplement, the employer knows they will be minimally supported. But if the employer's former employees utilize unemployment compensation, under most state systems, his contribution to the unemployment compensation system is increased. Thus the employer that "uses" AFDC instead of unemployment compensation can both pay low wages and save on the unemployment compensation taxes.

TABLE 5
The Dual Welfare System

Primary Welfare Sector	Secondary Welfare Sector
Benefit is a right.	Benefit is a privilege.
Coverage is universal, or at least general across eligible populations, e.g., all ex-soldiers are eligible, for veteran's benefits, over 95% of population reaching retirement age are covered by Social Security.	Coverage is only of certain segments of the population, such as income groups (means-tested programs), residents of poverty areas, members of race/ethnic groups (bilingual programs).
Receipt of services, or quality, not highly variable across country, often guaranteed by Federal Government, e.g., Medicare, unemployment compensation.	Quantity and quality of services is highly uneven and/or may depend on voluntary organizations such as churches, charities, women's groups; recipients include battered wives (services, shelters), rape victims, abused and neglected children.
Certainty, often including national standards, minimums and/or guarantees.	Uncertainty, local variations (e.g., whether one can find a doctor or hospital that will take Medicaid patients).
Benefits are often "fringes" of working and/or are tied to earnings (such as Social Security) and are viewed as "earned."	Benefits are tied to low income and/or receipt of welfare.
Privacy assured, no stigma.	Stigmatizing and publicly degrading, e.g., shopping with food stamps, forced cooperation in determining paternity.
Does not require "pauperization" to qualify, thus making it easier to use benefits to become upwardly mobile.	Requires pauperization (e.g., exhaustion of savings) to quality, making escape more difficult.
Higher average benefits levels including regular or frequent raises, and/or built-in "indexing."	Lower benefits levels, often below poverty level.
Benefit levels universal, with minimums.	Benefit levels highly variable by state and even locality; no Federal minimum or requirement of meeting a set percentage of state-determined need level.
Amount of benefits not reduced for unearned income; earned income taxed for retirees after first $5000.	Unearned income often deducted dollar for dollar, while earned income (for AFDC) after $360 annual work incentives taxed at rate of two-thirds.

These very different goals and patterns of services create two worlds differentiated by poverty rates, gender and race. Men, especially white men, are found disproportionately in the primary sector, while women and minorities are concentrated in the secondary sector. This division forces people to circulate between employment and unemployment *within* either the primary or the secondary sectors, but not *between* sectors, thus making permanent the inequality of opportunity and achievement between the two worlds.

In the primary sector, workers enjoy jobs with high pay and good fringe benefits, and if they do lose their jobs they are compensated relatively generously through unemployment compensation and/or union supplementary benefits. In contrast, in the secondary sector workers find themselves at relatively low-wage jobs with little job security and few fringe benefits. Should they lose their jobs—which happens relatively more frequently than in the primary sector, they may have to turn to public assistance. Indeed, AFDC functions as the poor woman's unemployment compensation.

Because such benefits as health care and child care are available only to these secondary workers through being "on welfare," many in this sector participate in both the labor market and the welfare system. This is especially true for women, and even more so for minority women. Although theoretically one could work one's way into the primary sector, in reality the secondary welfare and work sectors reinforce each other in a vicious circle, ensuring that workers in the secondary sector remain there.[73]

An example of the preferred treatment primary workers receive is the Trade Readjustment Act. Under its provisions, workers who are laid off or lose their jobs because of competitive imports receive up to 70 percent of their wages for up to 52 weeks. For example, 87 percent of union members in the auto industry, hard hit by imports, are men.

By contrast, for the increasing number of women homemakers who have been divorced, there is no provision allowing them a year-long search for a job, much less one at such highly remunerative rates. One evaluation of training programs for AFDC mothers focused on those who received their training in New York City and who were thus eligible for unemployment compensation if they did not find work. (In many locales, training programs are not counted as employment, even if they provide wage-level stipends.) The evaluation showed that women who received unemployment compensation remained unemployed longer than those who did not receive it. While

---

[72]Obviously, AFDC disproportionately "benefits" women, including many who are unemployed. But whether unemployment compensation, in terms of numbers and dollars, disproportionately benefits men cannot be determined with the statistics available as of this writing. The unavailability of even this basic information testifies to the "gender-blind" nature of welfare policy.

[73]Even the Federal Government reinforces the secondary status of women workers. In the program entitled While Actually Employed (WAE), which has the ostensible purpose of helping to ease the transition of women returning to the work world, women are "allowed" to work fewer than eight hours per day and to set their own hours. In return, they are paid minimum wage (though many have college degrees); are not paid on Federal holidays; and have no vacation, no lunch hour, no health or other "fringe" benefits, no promotional opportunities; and can be fired with one day's notice.

admitting that unemployment compensation might have made possible a longer job search resulting in a better job, the evaluators described it as having decreased the recipients' "work effort."[74]

The disparity in treatment between the primary and secondary sectors is more than a matter of remuneration or eligibility. It derives from fundamentally different conceptions of men workers and women workers: Men who are disadvantaged by factors such as imports and recessions should be compensated in a way that will facilitate their readjustment, via training, relocation and further education. That is, they have a "right" to the opportunity of good, self-supporting jobs. In contrast, women who are disadvantaged because of divorce, poor vocational training or preparation, or low education, should be helped—or forced—to take any job and any child day-care as quickly as possible, even if the job does not provide them with sufficient income to support themselves.

Toward a New Understanding of Women in Poverty

Women in poverty are workers. As workers they face specific gender-related barriers to full and equal participation in the labor force, and they require specific services to support that participation. If one considers homemaking and childrearing as work that is unpaid, nearly all "able-bodied" women are workers for most of their adult lives. As workers, women suffer a number of disadvantages that must be addressed if they are to achieve equal status and economic independence.

School and Socialization.   These disadvantages begin with a socialization process, which, through nonverbal pictures as well as the written and spoken word, sets forth limited goals and constrained opportunities for girls growing up.[75] Two general themes pervade the messages about vocational choices for girls. The future home and family are the first and primary occupation, and most women should enter occupations that are predominately female and low in authority, status and pay (in contrast to equivalent male occupations, e.g., nurse vs. doctor). Surprisingly, there has been little change in these messages in recent years. A mid-seventies study sought to find 10 secondary schools that were "pacesetters" in placing female students into nontraditional vocation tracks, but none could be found.[76] In 1980, in eight of the nine traditional areas of vocational education, 75 to 90 percent

---

[74]*Manpower Demonstration Research Corporation, Summary and Findings of the National Supported Work Demonstration,* (Cambridge, Mass.: Ballinger Publishing Co.) 1980.

[75]Women on Words and Images, *Dick and Jane as Victims: Sex Stereotyping in Children's Readers,* (Princeton, N.J.) 1975.

[76]Kathleen B. Boundy, "Sex Inequities in Education," *Clearinghouse Review,* Vol. 14, No. 11, February 1981.

of the students were men. (The exception is "distributive education," having to do with sales and distribution.)[77]

Even within a particular area of vocational education, women are disadvantaged. A study of a garment-industry vocational high school in New York City found that whites and males were disproportionately found in the highest of four tracks, in terms of pay and status, while women and minorities were overrepresented in the lowest.[78] Moreover, after graduation the latter groups were less successful in getting good paying jobs than those in the top track. Ironically, members in the top track often leave the field, ignoring their skills and getting jobs outside of the low-wage garment industry.[79]

In and Out of the Paid Labor Force. When women choose to leave paid work to become full-time homemakers and/or mothers, their disadvantages begin to multiply. First, this interruption of work experience is worsened because it usually occurs when earnings would be peaking, and in many occupations, it permanently sidetracks one from an upwardly mobile career ladder. Second, if a woman is disabled while out of the paid labor force, she is not eligible for disability insurance. Third, if a woman becomes a "displaced homemaker," as the increasing rates of divorce make more likely, she finds that her years of unpaid work, including volunteer work outside the home are given no value as "work experience" and are also held against her, particularly if her absence from the labor force has been quite long.

Finally, displaced homemakers and mothers attempting to re-enter the job market are often ineligible for unemployment compensation because they are not classified as "workers."

Child Day-Care. Quality child care is essential. Without the knowledge that one's children are being taken care of by responsible and loving people, it is impossible, logistically and psychologically, to work at a level that will result in economic self-sufficiency. Yet social welfare programs frustrate that objective by nonexistent or inconsistent support of day-care services.

Although relatives often provide the most trusted and preferred care, it is difficult to impossible to obtain reimbursement for such care. Publicly funded child day-care opportunities address only a small proportion of the need and may become scarce in the future. It is difficult to understand the lack of concern about adequate child day-care opportunities. Children are a society's future, and investment in them benefits society as a whole, as well as their mothers.

Breaking Down Barriers to Full and Equal Employment. Occupational segregation locks many women into jobs and careers that hold no

---

[77] *Ibid.*
[78] Baker, *op. cit.*
[79] *Ibid.*

potential for economic self-sufficiency. Designing and implementing programs that enable women, particularly those with low skills, minority status and other disadvantages, to enter male-dominated occupations requires much effort and perseverance. But almost two decades of experimentation and research have indicated that it can be done. The wall between the primary and secondary sector is not easily breached, but the alternative is to perpetuate the present system, a cruel hoax under which women are pushed to work yet are not allowed to achieve independence.

Conclusions

We live in a time of transition. More and more women are in charge of households and support their children alone or virtually alone. But even as their numbers are increasing, their economic status is not improving, so that many will be poor. This is true regardless of income source.

In spite of increased participation in the labor force, occupational segregation and discrimination have prevented improvement in women's earnings compared to those of men. Child support, which becomes more important as rates of divorce and illegitimacy increase, is so minimal that even the one- or two-child family runs a high risk of becoming poor if the father leaves. And welfare, though it supports a large percentage of the eligible population, does so at an even more penurious level than in the past.

The welfare system makes many women poor not only because its levels of payments are low, but also because it institutionalizes poverty for women. The pauperization processes of welfare unite and perpetuate inequality in the labor market, and women become locked into the secondary sectors of both the welfare system and the labor market. Such a system oppresses all women and endangers their economic well-being. The same work incentives that encourage women on welfare to work at poverty-level wages are also the means of subsidizing a low-wage labor force—which enables entire industries to pay poverty-level wages. Welfare programs that train and place poor women in traditionally female, low-wage jobs not only impoverish these women, but reinforce the barriers to primary-sector jobs for all women.

This need not be. If it is understood that the poverty women experience is fundamentally different from that experienced by men, it is possible to reorient policy and restructure programs. Clearly women do not lack the incentive to work. Rather, they encounter numerous disadvantages in the labor market and structural barriers to full and free participation. Appropriate programs must address these disadvantages at both the individual level (e.g., encouraging women to enter non-traditional occupations) and the institutional level (attacking sex discrimination, sex segregation and sexual harassment in organizations and industries).

Ways must be found to dismantle the dual welfare system and the dual labor market, which together lock women into permanent secondary status. Penurious welfare policies on the one hand and institutionalized underemployment on the other are trapping many women in a life of poverty. Unless we change our social welfare policies, we will continue to build, for increasing numbers of women, a "workhouse without walls."

POVERTY IN AMERICA:
MYTHS AND REALITIES 1981[80]

When the Council, in last year's *Twelfth Report*, asked how much progress had been made toward diminishing poverty since the "War on Poverty" began in the 1960's, the answers found were not encouraging. Contrary to the optimistic claims of some official and academic commentators, our evidence demonstrated that, in many ways, the problems of poverty deepened during the 1970's—and that the outlook for the near future did not seem promising.

Unfortunately, that general picture has changed only slightly since last year; and the change has been for the worse. According to U.S. Bureau of the Census estimates, over 700,000 more Americans were poor in 1979 than in 1978. That overall increase included significant rises in poverty among two groups whose situations had been improving steadily in recent years: the aged; and black, married-couple families.[81] These negative developments, resulting from the impact of recession and inflation on jobs and living standards, have convinced the Council that the analyses and conclusions of last year's *Report* are as timely and urgent as ever. The Council therefore decided to prepare an expanded and updated analysis of the myths and realities of poverty, which considers new information and the most recent available statistics.

How much progress has been made toward diminishing poverty in America since the signing of the Economic Opportunity Act of 1964 and the declaration of a national "War on Poverty"?

The official poverty count figures from the U.S. Bureau of the Census

---

[80]This Chapter updates and revises a section of the *Twelfth Report* by the National Advisory Council on Economic Opportunity, Washington, D.C., 1980.

[81]*Money Income and Poverty Status of Families and Persons in the United States* (Advance Report), in *Current Population Reports*, (Washington, D.C.: U.S. Department of Commerce, Bureau of the Census). Series P-60, No. 125, 1979, pp. 3-4. *The Council stresses throughout this Report that the official poverty figures do not adequately describe the much larger number of people whose incomes cannot support a minimal standard of living, or who live so close to the poverty line that they are in constant danger of falling below it. A study by the University of Michigan, for example, suggests that one in every four Americans fall below official poverty levels at some point over a nine-year period. About 55 million Americans by this calculation now live precariously close to poverty.* On these issues see University Survey Research Center, *Five Thousand American Families: Patterns of Economic Progress,* Vol. II, 1975, pp. 33-35; and Sar A. Levitan, *Programs in Aid of the Poor for the 1980's,* (Baltimore, Md.: John Hopkins University Press) 1980, pp. 5-8. *Later in this chapter, some of the issues surrounding the definition and measurement of poverty will be discussed in detail.*

provide one not very encouraging answer: As of 1979, more than 25 million Americans were poor—considerably fewer than the 36 million who were poor in 1964, but amounting to almost 12 percent of the population, a rate that has remained depressingly stable for over a decade.[82]

The Myth

Yet, in the past few years a different a wholly misleading answer has become increasingly fashionable. Many economists and social scientists (as well as other observers in the universities, in government and in the private sector) have argued that the War on Poverty has, essentially, been won; and all that remain are a few minor skirmishes. In 1976, University of Virginia economist Edgar K. Browning wrote in *The Public Interest* magazine that "there is practically no poverty, statistically speaking, in the United States today, and indeed there has not been for several years."[83] In the same year, the United States Chamber of Commerce asked, "Have we licked poverty without knowing it.?"[84] Even some serious students of the poverty problem began to argue that "the day of income poverty as a major public issue would appear to be past."[85] By 1978, Martin Anderson of the Hoover Institution, and currently Assistant to the President for Policy Development, declared flatly that:

> The "War on Poverty" that began in 1964 has been won; the growth of jobs and income in the private economy, combined with an explosive increase in government spending and income transfer programs, has virtually eliminated poverty in the United States.[86]

The notion that poverty in America has been abolished, for all practical purposes, has by now acquired the status of a new myth—one with profound implications for social policy. For if poverty has been eliminated, it obviously makes little sense to increase spending on programs that benefit the poor, since, as one economist has argued, "an inadequate level of benefits for the poor is no longer a pressing issue."[87] This myth further suggests, as Edgar Browning put it in 1976, that we have achieved all the income equality we can "afford"; that any more redistribution of income to the

---

[82]*Ibid.* p. 29.

[83]Edgar K. Browning, "How Much More Equality Can We Afford?", *The Public Interest,* Spring 1976, p. 92.

[84]Carl Madden, *A Look at the U.S. Income Distribution: Have We Licked Poverty Without Knowing It?,* (Washington, D.C.: U.S. Chamber of Commerce) March 1976.

[85]Robert H. Haveman, "Poverty and Social Policy in the 1960's and 1970's—an Overview and Some Speculations," in Robert H. Haveman, ed., *A Decade of Federal Anti-Poverty Programs,* (New York: Academic Press) 1977, p. 18.

[86]Martin Anderson, *Welfare,* Standard: Hoover Institution Press) 1978, p. 15.

[87]Edgar K. Browning, "Welfare: A Reconstruction," *The Humanist,* March/April 1977, p. 14.

disadvantaged, in this view, would result in serious "disincentives" for the affluent.[88]

At the extreme, the myth lends itself to the idea that we should dismantle parts of the existing system of benefits to the poor in favor of letting "market forces" have more influence in determining their well-being. More generally, the myth of the "abolition of poverty" supports those who favor a shift of resources and concern away from the poor and the public sector, toward the presumed needs of the private economy for greater capital investment— a shift away from social programs toward the accumulation of private wealth.

The myth of the "abolition of poverty" is appealing in an age of slow economic growth and tight budgets. And, like most myths, it has its own kernel of truth. There have been significant gains in the battle against poverty, but the successes have been much less dramatic, and the losses much more serious, than the myth suggests. It exaggerates, first, the beneficial impact of recent economic growth on poverty; and second, the effectiveness of welfare and income transfers in providing a cushion for those whom economic growth has left behind.

The Realities

The evidence shows that poverty is not only still with us, but that it is also increasingly immune to the remedies of the past. And although some groups have fared relatively well under the antipoverty strategies of the past decade and a half, others have not. More specifically, a fair and realistic interpretation of the facts would show that:

- Poverty has been only minimally reduced since the late 1960's; moreover, any improvement in the past decade has resulted almost entirely from the expansion of "income transfer" and Federal antipoverty programs.[89] The kind of economic growth promoted in the past 10 years has not significantly improved the opportunities of the poor for decent, permanent jobs and adequate earnings.
- The pattern of recent economic development has created a vast population of the economically marginal and welfare dependent. Many have been lifted above the official poverty threshold by social insurance and welfare transfers, but many have not. Of those who have, many, even under the most generous definitions, have not been raised to what the U.S. Department of Labor defines as a "lower living standard."
- Although the poverty count has dropped in the past decade and a half, the poverty population is less equally distributed than in the mid-1960's. Measured by their relative chances of being poor, the most

---

[88]*Cf.* Browning, "Equality," *passim.*

[89]These include social service and economic development programs provided for by the Economic Opportunity Act of 1964.

traditionally disadvantaged groups in American society—minorities and women—are worse off than a decade ago. If one main objective of the War on Poverty has been to achieve racial and sexual equality of opportunity, we are losing—and losing badly.

The following sections explore these issues. The first gives an overview of what the official Census data and a number of recent studies reveal about current trends in poverty in America. Much of the new myth of the "abolition of poverty" is based on criticism of the adequacy of the official data, however; the second section evaluates that critique and assesses how much it should shift our understanding of the scope of poverty today. Finally, a third section offers some general conclusions and suggestions for public policy.

Patterns of Poverty

Stagnation and Uneven Development. Two facts stand out with respect to the broad contours of poverty in the United States over the past two decades—as measured by the Census Bureau. First, although poverty rates declined significantly in the early 1960's, the reduction in poverty had ground almost to a halt by the end of that decade. Second, even in the earlier period, the reduction in poverty was mainly confined to certain regions and not to others.

In 1959, a little over 22 percent of the American population was poor; by 1969, only 12 percent was poor. But the next several years brought virtually no change in overall poverty rates, which rose during the recession of 1975 over their 1969 level and, even in the "recovery" year of 1978, arrived at a level only about one-half of one percentage point below it—only to rise again as recession began once more in 1979.[90]

But that general pattern masks a fact that is less often recognized: Most of the reduction in poverty, even during the economic expansion of the 1960's, occurred in the South, and, to an even greater degree, generally in rural areas. In the North and West, especially in cities, poverty has proven more resistant from the start.

Of the approximately 14 million fewer poor in 1979 than in 1959, nine million were Southern. Between 1969 and 1979, the *number* of poor people in the North and West rose by one and one half million. Even more striking, the *rate* of poverty in the North and West has *risen* since 1969, while the Southern rate has fallen. That rise has been concentrated in the Northeastern

---

[90]In 1979, the poverty rate for persons of all races was 11.6 percent—a slight rise over the 1978 rate of 11.4 percent. Black poverty—officially 30.9 percent in 1979—was only a little over one percentage point lower than in 1969. Comparable data on poverty among Americans of Spanish origin has been collected only since 1972, but the overall pattern is clearly the same. The rate of poverty among Hispanics (21.6 percent in 1979) was just over one-half a percentage point below the level of seven years earlier. *Money Income and Poverty Status, op. cit.*, p. 29.

states, where the rate of poverty rose by 20 percent between 1969 and 1979.[91]

The decline in poverty among Southern blacks highlights the North-South difference even more strongly. At the end of the 1950's, over two-thirds of the black population in the South was poor; by 1979, only one-third. But the rate of poverty among Northern blacks, after nearly two decades of economic growth and civil rights legislation, has declined only marginally in 20 years. There are one million more black poor in the Northern and Western states today than in 1959.[92]

In part, the persistence of poverty among Northern blacks reflects the massive migration of poor blacks out of the South during the post-World War II period.[93] But it also indicates the resistance of the kind of poverty suffered by Northern blacks to antipoverty strategies and economic growth. Much the same picture emerges, too, for the Hispanic poor. Poverty among Americans of Spanish origin rose sharply in the 1970's in New England and in the Midwest (and almost as much in the Pacific region), while it declined in the Southern and Mountain states.[94]

The resistance of Northern poverty is closely bound up with the greater intractability of *urban* poverty in general. Just as the "successes" in the War on Poverty have been mostly in the South, so too have they been mainly rural. Of those 14 million fewer poor since 1959, about 12 million were accounted for by nonmetropolitan areas. Central-city poverty, on the other hand, has declined only slightly since 1959, and has *risen* during the 1970's. For both races, but especially for blacks, central-city rates of family poverty were higher in 1979 than a decade earlier.[95] The most striking increases

---

[91]The poverty rate in the Northeastern states was 8.6 percent in 1969, and 10.3 percent in 1979. *Money Income and Poverty Status*, p. 33; and *Characteristics of the Population Below the Poverty Level*, in *Current Population Reports*, (Washington, D.C.: U.S. Department of Commerce, Bureau of the Census). Series P-60, No. 124, 1978, p. 24.

[92]The poverty rate for Northern blacks started lower—34 percent in 1959—but fell to only 28 percent in 1979. *Money Income and Poverty Status*, p. 33; and *Characteristics of the Population*, pp. 24-25.

[93]That pattern began to shift in the late 1960's, so that today the South has more poor moving in than moving out. See Larry H. Long, "Interregional Migration of the Poor: Some Recent Changes," (Washington, D.C.: U.S. Department of Commerce, Bureau of the Census) 1978.

[94]Data from the 1976 Survey of Income and Education—which are not strictly comparable to the annual *Current Population Reports*—show that between 1969 and 1975, the rate of poverty among families of Spanish origin rose from 17.3 percent to 33.8 percent in New England; from 11.7 percent to 18.4 percent in the North Central states; and from 14.1 percent to 18.4 percent in the Pacific states. Their rate of poverty declined—although only very slightly—in the Mountain states (from 23.5 percent to 21.0 percent) and somewhat more in the West South Central states (30.7 percent to 25.7 percent). *Demographic, Social, and Economic Profit of States*, in *Current Population Reports*, (Washington, D.C.: U.S. Department of Commerce, Bureau of the Census). Series P-20, No. 334, 1976.

[95]The poverty rate among families in central cities was 13.7 percent in 1959, dropped to 9.8 percent in 1969, and rose back to 12.6 percent in 1979. Among black families, the central-city poverty rate was 34.3 percent in 1959, 21.5 percent in 1969 and 28.5 percent in 1979. *Characteristics of the Population, op. cit.*, pp. 21-22; and *Money Income and Poverty Status, op. cit.*, p. 36.

in big-city poverty, not surprisingly, have been in the Northeastern and Midwestern cities especially hard-hit by regional economic decline. Thus, according to U.S. Department of Housing and Urban Development data, New York City's poverty rate jumped by about 25 percent between the end of the 1960's and the late 1970's; Philadelphia's by 38 percent; and Chicago's by 47 percent. Overall, "needy" cities—those suffering economic and population decline—averaged an increase of almost one-third in rates of poverty in those years.[96]

The stagnation in national poverty rates, and the increasing concentration of the poor in central cities of the North and West, suggests that the development of the American economy in the recent past has had a highly uneven impact on patterns of poverty. This becomes clearer when we look more specifically at the shifting role of economic growth in reducing poverty.

The Declining Impact of Growth in the Private Sector. As we have seen, the basic premise of those who argue that poverty has been "abolished" is that "the growth of jobs and income in the private economy" has been a main force in reducing poverty to "minor" proportions. The general implication is that our recent macroeconomic policy has worked well in alleviating the plight of the disadvantaged. This myth vindicates the hopes of those who believe that poverty will be almost automatically reduced through the "trickling down" of jobs and earnings from a dynamic private economy. But a careful look at both the Census data and the results of recent special studies suggests that just the opposite is true. On the contrary, the private economy has done little by way of jobs and earnings for the poor since the mid-1960's. Although economic growth did improve the situation of some groups of the poor before that time, it has since had a dwindling impact. *Virtually all of the reduction in poverty since the mid-1960's has come about through the expansion of social insurance and income transfer programs.*

One way of looking at this is by comparing rates of poverty before and after income from transfers is counted. The Census poverty measure includes income from transfers. "Pre-transfer" poverty, on the other hand, is a rough but useful measure of how well the economy is managing to put people to work at living wages. About 21 percent of Americans, according to Census data, were poor before transfers in 1965; about 21 percent were poor before transfers in 1976.

Many of those pre-transfer poor are aged, and it might seem that the complete stagnation in the rate of pre-transfer poverty since 1965 reflects a greater proportion of the aged being counted. But the same flat poverty rate applies to the non-aged as well. In 1965, and again in 1976, about 16 percent of people in non-aged households were poor before government

---

[96] *The President's National Urban Policy Report, 1980*, (Washington, D.C.: U.S. Department of Housing and Urban Development) Table 4–5, pp. 4–8.

transfers.[97] About one in five Americans, then, lives in a household that depends on income other than earnings for a subsistence living; of those living in non-aged households, the proportion is a little under one in six. These proportions have not changed since the mid-1960's.

The implication—that there has been little noticeable improvement in the labor-market situation of the poor—is borne out by more elaborate studies. A recent analysis for the Office of Income Security Policy of the Department of Health, Education and Welfare (HEW) found that, between 1967 and 1973, the incidence of what the study calls "earnings poverty"—poverty before income transfers—actually increased, although the overall Census poverty count fell significantly. In other words, the ability of people to raise themselves above the poverty line through work alone *declined* during that period; it was income transfers, not jobs, that pulled people out of poverty. Surprisingly, the HEW study found that "earnings poverty" increased not only among families headed by women and the aged (which one would expect to be less affected by economic growth), but also for families headed by non-aged males. Although average earnings for men as a whole rose during that period, the incidence of *inadequate* earnings among prime-aged men rose as well, suggesting a deepening split between those with good earning power and those without.[98]

The HEW study concludes that "poverty will not continue to decline at the rate experienced in the late 1960's and early 1970's unless transfer payments continue to expand."[99] Much the same conclusion emerges from a University of Delaware study of the impact of economic growth on poverty rates. The study divided the post-war period into two parts, 1947–63 and 1964–74, and found that while economic growth had a strong impact on reducing the poverty count in the first period, it had little impact in the second. After 1964, moreover, economic growth was responsible for reducing poverty almost wholly among male-headed families; both minorities and women were virtually unaffected by the "trickling down" of economic growth into improved jobs and earnings.[100]

The stubborn persistence of poverty even in areas of rapid growth in employment and income offers further evidence of the limits of conventional economic growth in reducing modern urban poverty. We have seen that the sharpest increases in poverty during the 1970's were in the hard-hit, declining cities of the Northeast and Midwest. But poverty rates also remained

---

[97]Sheldon Danziger and Robert Plotnick, *Can Welfare Reform Eliminate Poverty?*, Discussion Paper No. 517-78, Institute for Research on Poverty, (Madison, Wisc.: University of Wisconsin) August 1978, p. 13.

[98]Peter Gottschalk, *Earnings, Transfers, and Poverty Reduction*, Technical Paper No. 16, (Washington, D.C.: Department of Health, Education and Welfare, Office of Income Security Policy) October 1978. The official poverty rate fell from 14.2 percent to 11.1 percent from 1967 to 1973.

[99]*Ibid.*, p. 53

[100]James R. Thornton, Richard J. Agnello and Charles R. Lind, "Poverty and Economic Growth: Trickle Down Peters Out," *Economic Inquiry*, July 1978.

disturbingly stable even in those cities characterized by strong—occasionally phenomenal—growth in jobs and income. Thus, cities described by HUD as having "low to moderate" need—with relatively rapid annual growth in jobs, income and population—had an average poverty rate of 12.2 percent in 1969. By 1977, that rate had fallen imperceptibly to 11.7 percent. In Houston, where annual job growth averaged an astonishingly high 6 percent from 1970 to 1977, the official poverty rate declined only slightly—from 14 percent in 1969 to 12.2 percent in 1976-78. Moreover, whether any significant part of that minor decline was the result of improved opportunities for jobs and earnings—rather than simply the result of improved transfer benefits—is unclear. In short, economic growth has had little impact in decreasing poverty rates in recent years, even in the boom cities of the "Sunbelt."[101]

Still another view of the decreasing role of improvements in jobs and earnings appears if we examine the Census evidence on the work experience of those people who *have* crossed the poverty threshold during the past decade. Census estimates of family poverty, broken down by the number of workers in the family, reveal a significant pattern.[102]

Between 1959 and 1967, during the economic expansion of he 1960's, the rate of poverty dropped much faster for families with one paid worker— which fit most closely with the conventional idea of the working poor—than for families with no workers outside the home. But after 1967 the pattern reversed. The rate of poverty among families with one paid worker fell only slightly, while the rate for families with no paid workers dropped considerably. At the same time, in an apparent paradox, families without paid workers became a larger *proportion* of the poverty population; one-worker families are now a somewhat smaller proportion of the poor. The reason for this seeming paradox is simple—but not encouraging. The *overall* number of families without paid workers has risen sharply in recent years. Many such families have risen above the official poverty lines by means of income transfers, which account for their declining *rate* of poverty. But a substantial— and growing—number have not, which accounts for their rising presence in the poverty population.[103]

Since the late 1960's, then, our pattern of economic growth has had little impact on the lot of the working poor—and only an indirect impact, through

---

[101] *The President's National Urban Policy Report, 1980,* (Washington, D.C.: U.S. Department of Housing and Urban Development) Table 4-5, pp. 4-8.

[102] The Bureau of the Census' use of the term "worker" is somewhat misleading (since it implies that those who are not paid employees are "non-workers"), particularly since many women who are not members of the *paid* labor force do, of course, work—at unpaid labor in the home. This *Report* retains the Census' usage for the sake of continuity.

[103] In 1979, 1.7 times as many white families included no paid workers as in 1969; among blacks the number more than doubled. More than one-third of Puerto Rican families in the mainland U.S. have no paid workers. Some of this change reflects a somewhat larger population of people over 65 in the population. Data calculated from *Characteristics of the Population, op. cit.,* p. 32; and *Money Income and Poverty Status, op. cit.,* p. 34.

increased welfare and social insurance benefits, on the non-working poor. It has left us with both a fairly stable population of those who work more or less regularly but cannot earn enough to live decently, and a growing population of those who have been effectively excluded from regular work altogether.

The Changing Faces of Poverty. Only the expansion of income transfers and social insurance has kept the poverty population from—at best—remaining at the same level as in 1967. But the stubborn persistence of overall poverty rates since the late 1960's has not meant that the *contours* of poverty have been unchanged. As in a game of musical chairs, the poor have been shifted around; the size of the poverty population has not changed much, but its composition has. Some groups have fared much better than others over the past decade; two patterns in particular stand out.

First, the age distribution of the officially poor has shifted. Today's poor are less often the aged, more often the young—especially very young children. At the same time, the continuing hardship of the low-income aged shows quite clearly the limited effect of the welfare state, even for those usually defined as relative "winners" in the War on Poverty. And recent increases in poverty rates for the over-65 indicate the continued vulnerability of the aged to changes in economic conditions and public policy.

Second, whatever progress we have made in reducing overall poverty levels in the past 10 years has been accompanied by increased sexual and racial inequality.

The Old and the Young. The aged are widely thought to be the "success story" of the War on Poverty. Their official poverty rate, in 1978, was still above that of the population as a whole, but only a little more than one-half of what it had been a decade earlier. There were still about 300,000 more poor Americans in 1978 than 10 years earlier. But over the same period, the number of aged poor dropped by more than one and one-half million.[104]

Clearly, the elderly benefitted the most from the expansion of the services of the welfare state, notably Social Security Insurance, during the 1970's—indeed, the elderly account for much of the decrease in official poverty rates during the decade. But the implication that poverty among the aged has been nearly eliminated, or that their living standards have dramatically improved, is cruelly misleading.

First, poverty among the aged increased significantly from 1978 to 1979—an illustration of the precarious situation of many older people in the face of economic downturn and a harsher climate of public policy. The number of aged poor increased by an estimated 350,000—the first such rise since the recession of 1974–75.[105]

---

[104]In 1978, persons 65 and over had an official poverty rate of 14.0 percent. *Money Income and Poverty Status, op. cit.*, p. 29.

[105]*Ibid.*, p. 3.

Second, the reduction in official poverty has been very uneven among different groups of the aged, just as it has been in the population as a whole. More than one in four elderly Hispanics and over one in three elderly blacks were poor in 1979, and the pace of improvement for both has been much slower over the last decade than for the white aged.[106]

The condition of the aged also depends crucially on sex and family status. Older women face much higher risks of poverty than do older men, and both are much more likely to be poor if they are living alone—"unrelated individuals," in the language of the Census. In 1976, as a recent Social Security Administration study shows, almost two out of five nonmarried women over 65 were poor, compared with a little more than one quarter of elderly nonmarried men, and less than one in 10 elderly married individuals.[107]

When the disadvantages of race, sex and family status are combined, the poverty rates of the aged rise to appalling levels. More than two out of five elderly black women are poor; more than three out of five if they are "unrelated individuals."[108]

Third—as is true for many others of the poor—many of the aged who have officially "moved out" of poverty have not moved far, and still live precariously close to the poverty line. This is especially true of those of the aged whose livelihoods are entirely dependent on public transfers. In 1977, aged "unrelated individuals" whose only source of income was Social Security benefits were more likely to be poor than not, for their median income was more than $100 below the poverty threshold. But even for those aged who can combine more than one source of income, the distance from official poverty is short, unless they are fortunate enough to still have income from earnings. In 1977, the median income for individuals 65 and over who lived solely on income other than earnings was only about $700 above the poverty line; this income includes not just public transfer payments but private pensions and income from property as well.[109]

As this information suggests, beneath the appearance of a dramatic decline in poverty among the aged is the reality that most of those who have "moved out" of poverty have, in fact, moved from a few hundred dollars below the poverty line to only a few hundred dollars above it. This is confirmed, from another vantage point, if we add to the officially poor those of the aged whose incomes fall below 125 percent of the poverty level—a threshold which was roughly $600 below the U.S. Bureau of Labor Statistics' "lower budget" for an urban retired couple in 1978. About one-fourth of the aged fall into this expanded category—about 1.7 times the proportion who are officially

---

[106]*Ibid.*, p. 29.

[107]Susan Grad and Karen Foster, "Income of the Population Aged 65 and Over," *Social Security Bulletin,* July 1979.

[108]*Money Income and Poverty, op. cit.,* p. 33; and *Characteristics of the Population, op. cit.,* p. 23.

[109]*Social and Economic Characteristics of the Older Population,* in *Current Population Reports,* (Washington, D.C.: U.S. Department of Commerce, Bureau of the Census). Series P-23, No. 85, 1978, p. 32.

poor—as do two-fifths of the aged in female-headed families, half of the black aged, and two-thirds of the black aged in female-headed families.[110]

A recent analysis of the cost of necessities in New Jersey found that the Federal poverty thresholds, as of 1980, amounted to only 70 percent of what an elderly couple would need to sustain life on a *minimally* adequate budget: With Social Security payments *and* Food Stamps, the couple would receive only 79 percent of the income necessary to maintain that minimal standard of living.[111]

If the record of combatting the poverty of the elderly in America is not nearly so bright as it has sometimes been pictured, the growth in poverty among the very young has been one of the major social disasters of the 1970's—one that went largely unnoticed.

As the number of aged who are officially poor dropped, the number of poor youth rose. There were close to 200,000 more poor children under 18 in 1979 than in 1969. Their rate of poverty rose by more than 15 percent in those years. Predictably, minority children face the greatest risks of poverty. More than one in four Hispanic children and about two in five black children were poor in 1978.[112]

But these statistics, covering the nation as a whole, actually minimize the growing crisis of youthful poverty in the urban-industrial North and West. We have already noted how poverty in the Northern and Western cities has proven highly resistant to both economic growth and antipoverty strategies. For young children, the pattern is even more alarming.

Data from the 1976 Survey of Income and Education show that, while the nationwide poverty rate for youth under 18 changed little between 1969 and 1975, it shot up rapidly—by 17 percent and 18 percent, respectively—in the North-Eastern and North-Central states, with some states registering much sharper increases. It is especially ominous that the spread of youth poverty in the North has been most rapid among the youngest children. The poverty rate among related children under five rose about 12 percent nationally between 1969 and 1975.[113] But it rose by 49 percent in New Jersey, 56 percent in Michigan, 58 percent in Illinois, and an astonishing 68 percent in Ohio in those few years.[114]

---

[110]*Money Income and Poverty Status, op. cit.,* p. 32.

[111]*The Cost of an Adequate Living Standard in New Jersey,* (Washington, D.C.: National Social Science and Law Project) 1980, pp. 16, 18.

[112]All these figures refer to related children under 18. The 1979 rate for related children under 18 was 15.9 percent, compared with 13.8 percent in 1969. By contrast, the rate for those aged 22 to 44 was 8.2 percent. Ominously, the rate for the youngest children is the highest—18.2 percent for those under 3. *Money Income and Poverty Status, op. cit.,* pp. 29, 33.

[113]According to the Bureau of the Census, related children include own children and all other children in the household who are related to the family head by blood, marriage or adoption.

[114]The national rate of poverty for related children under 18 was 15.8 percent in 1969 and 15.3 percent in 1975, according to this survey. These figures differ somewhat from those in the annual Consumer Income Surveys, since they are based on different samples. There were 100,000 more poor children in just the combined states of Ohio and Illinois in 1975 than in 1969. *Demographic, Social and Economic Profile, op. cit.,* pp. 68–69.

The Growth of Inequality. Beneath the myth of the "abolition of poverty," then, is the reality of continuing hardship for the aged and a shocking increase in poverty among youth—especially the children of the inner cities. But progress against poverty has differed not only according to age, but according to sex and race as well.

To the extent that there have been "winners" in the War on Poverty during the 1970's, they have been male—and mainly white. What one writer has called the "feminization of poverty" has become one of the most compelling social facts of the decade. And at the same time, relatedly, the chances of poverty have also increased for blacks, relative to whites.[115]

The shift toward an increasing proportion of women (and children in families with a female householder) among the poor has been disturbingly rapid. In 1976, they passed men (and children in male-householder families) in absolute numbers, and this trend has continued. Almost one female-householder family in three is poor; about one in 19 families with a male householder is poor. The decline in poverty during the past decade has been almost entirely in male-householder families. In 1979, there were over 1 million fewer poor children in families with a male householder than in 1969. But there were more than 1.2 million *more* poor children in families with a female householder.[116]

The main source of this startling shift has been the rising frequency of marital disruption, coupled with women's continuingly poor opportunities for decent earnings and the lack of adequate benefits and supportive services for single women with children. In 1978, one in five families in the U.S. had a single parent, compared to one in nine in 1970. Most of those single parents are women, and their risks of poverty are almost three times that of single fathers—whose poverty rate, in turn, is more than twice that of married householders with children.

As in the case of the aged, the broad statistics mask two key facts about the state of single mothers: Even those who are not poor by official measures are often not far from poverty; and those who also face the burdens of youth and/or minority status are much worse off than others. Two-thirds of women householders under 25 with children were poor in 1978—almost three out of four for blacks.[117]

The crippling poverty of single mothers reflects both their exclusion from

---

[115]*Cf.* Diana Pearce, *The Feminization of Poverty—Women, Work, and Welfare* (Unpublished manuscript, Department of Sociology, University of Illinois, Chicago Circle) 1978.

[116]*Money Income and Poverty Status, op. cit.,* Table 18, pp. 30–31. Beginning in 1979, the Census Bureau no longer uses the terms "male-headed" or "female-headed" families. To avoid the bias implicit in the concept of "heading" families, the Census Bureau now uses the terms "families with a male (or with a female) householder." In most cases, this usage has no effect, or only a slight effect, on the calculation of poverty rates. In this *Report*, we use the new "householder" terminology, except when referring to certain earlier studies or data where use of the newer terms might be confusing. For a detailed discussion of terminology changes, see *Characteristics of the Population, op. cit.,* Introduction.

[117]*Ibid.,* p. 86.

steady work and the rock-bottom earnings they often receive even when working regularly. The majority of female householders with children work in the paid labor force at some point during the year, and they fare much better than those who are entirely dependent on income transfers for a living. Nine out of ten single mothers with children under six who did not work (in the paid labor force) during 1978 were below the poverty line—another comment on the limits of our supposedly ''over-generous'' welfare system. But women's earnings are often so low that even full-time work is no security against poverty: One-third of female householders with children under six who worked *full-time* at some point in 1978 were poor—including one in every 10 working full-time and year-round.[118]

The much more rapid decline in poverty for men has meant that the inequality in life-chances between men and women has grown considerably over the past few years. At the end of the 1960's, women faced a much greater risk of poverty than men; in the 1970's, that disparity became even greater. In 1967, a female householder was about 3.8 times more likely to be poor than a male householder. By 1979, after more than a decade of anti-discrimination efforts, she was about 5.5 times more likely to be poor.[119] If anything, the evidence suggests that this trend will continue to worsen. One indication is that the income gap between the sexes, widest among the young, has grown still wider in recent years. A young (under 25) female householder in 1967 was about 5 times more likely than a young man to be poor; by 1978, eight times.[120] It is among the rising generation of young women, then, that the poverty of the 1970's has been most devastating, and that the outlook for the 1980's is most bleak.

We have already noted that poverty has become increasingly concentrated in central cities. A closer look at the figures reveals that the increase in central-city poverty rates has been entirely among female householder families: Poverty among families with a male householder declined in the inner cities during the 1970's (by almost 23 percent from 1969 to 1978). But the poverty rate among families with a female householder rose by 14 percent in central cities in the same years.[121]

The deepening inequality between men and women is compounded, predictably, when joined with the division between minority and white: The poverty population is becoming more minority as it becomes more female. The pace of change is not as fast for minorities as it is for women, but the rate of change is significant. In 1969, the rate of poverty among black householders was roughly 3.6 times that of whites. By 1979, it was four times the white rate.

---

[118]*Ibid.*, pp. 30–31. Comparable poverty rates for male householders with children under six were 5.7 percent for some full-time work, 3.5 percent for year-round full-time work. The number of single parents in poverty would be much higher if the cost of day care had been considered in determining actual income.

[119]Calculated from *Money Income and Poverty Status, Ibid.*, pp. 30–31.

[120]*Current Population Reports* (Washington, D.C.: U.S. Department of Commerce, Bureau of the Census). Series P-60, No. 119, p. 30; and *Characteristics of the Population, op. cit.*, p. 33.

[121]*Characteristics of the Population, op. cit.*, p. 7.

That increase may seem fairly small, but its significance becomes clearer when we consider that it is only a relatively sharp drop in poverty rates for black male householder families that has kept black poverty rates from leaping still faster ahead of the rates for whites. The relative situation of black women has deteriorated sharply in the past decade. This is particularly apparent if we compare their poverty rates with those of white males. In 1967, a black female householder had 7.5 times the chance of being poor as did a white male; by 1979 she had more than 10 times the chance.[122]

The growth of the welfare state since the late 1960's, therefore, has had a critical impact on the shape of poverty in America. But that impact has had less to do with reducing the size of the poverty population, than with shifting the sex (and, to a lesser degree, the color) of the people within it. All other things being equal, if the proportion of the poor in female-householder families were to continue to increase at the same rate as it did from 1967 to 1978, the poverty population would be composed solely of women and their children before the year 2000.[123]

The Impact of "In-Kind" Benefits

The stalemate in the War on Poverty in the 1970's occurred in spite of the greatest increase in government spending on programs for the poor in our history. That apparent paradox has spurred a number of attempts, beginning in the mid-1970's, to show that the official statistics collected by the Federal Government have inadequately measured the real economic well-being of the poor—and that such statistics have particularly undervalued the contribution of our expanded welfare system in improving the condition of the poor.

These studies are the heart of the new myth of the "abolition of poverty." They argue that the main reason poverty has not declined in recent years, despite massive welfare spending, is that the official poverty measure counts only the *money* income of the poor. Since the end of the 1960's, however, the fastest-growing category of aid to the poor has been the so-called "in-kind" benefits—chiefly medical and housing subsidies and Food Stamps. Because these benefits are not in the form of cash payments, they are not counted as income by the Census, although, in this argument, they have greatly added to the effective income of the poor.

---

[122]*Money Income and Poverty Status, op. cit.,* pp. 29–31. Between 1967 and 1979, the poverty rate for black female householders dropped by only 13 percent (from 56 percent to 49 percent) while that for black male householders was cut almost in half (from 25 percent to 13 percent). Hispanic female householders have the same poverty ratio to white males as do black females— roughly half of Hispanic female householders are below the poverty level, compared to about one in 20 white male householders.

[123]Based on *Characteristocs of the Population, op. cit.,* pp. 16–18. Persons in female households were about 38 percent of the total poor in 1967, and 53 percent in 1978; or an increase by about 39 percent over their 1967 proportion. To reduce confusion, we should stress that this is not a prediction of what the poverty population will actually look like in the year 2000—but rather an illustration of the magnitude and speed of the "feminization of poverty" in recent years.

One early study argued that if in-kind benefits were included, the poverty population had, for all practical purposes, disappeared by the mid-1970's, and "it only remains for our accounting procedures to be modified to record this achievement."[124] Studies by the Congressional Budget Office (CBO) and the University of Wisconsin's Institute for Research on Poverty came to less sweeping but generally similar conclusions. The CBO study, for example, adjusted the Census data to account both for the value of in-kind transfers and for the impact of taxes on the poor's income. Where the Census, in fiscal year 1976, had found about 13.5 percent of American families in poverty, the CBO's measure reduced the figure to 8.3 percent.

On the same principle, since the volume of in-kind transfers had increased so much in recent years, there had been (in that view) a much faster *reduction* in poverty—about 66 percent since 1965, according to the CBO, versus the more modest estimate of 28 percent in the official Census figures. The CBO's conclusion was that "if income is examined after taxes and after transfers, there has been marked progress in reducing the incidence of poverty among families."[125]

The Wisconsin studies also estimated the value of in-kind transfers and taxes in the poor's income and, in addition, attempted to account for the under-reporting of income by the poor, and other technical problems in income measurement. On that basis, Timothy Smeeding calculated that the actual rate of poverty in 1972 was only about 6.6 percent of all households, versus the Census Bureau's reported 14.6 percent. And Smeeding contended that these adjustments meant that poverty had been reduced by about 39 percent (versus the Census' 7.6 percent) since 1968. By this accounting, in other words, the Census' poverty count should be halved and the rate of progress in reducing poverty quintupled.[126]

Obviously, these revisions of the official poverty count could have profound implications for our understanding of poverty and the policies we devise to deal with it. How accurate are they? The issues are complex, and made more so because discussions of the measurement of poverty have been recorded in obscure journals and technical reports, and couched in forbiddingly technical jargon.

Moreover, two kinds of issues are involved in assessing the significance of the argument regarding in-kind income. Some are simply technical ones of measurement; others are broader and deeper questions about how we choose to *define* poverty and what we want the definition to accomplish. On both

---

[124]Browning, "Equality," *op. cit.,* p. 92.

[125]Congressional Budget Office, *Poverty Status of Families Under Alternative Definitions of Income,* Background Paper No. 17, Revised, (Washington, D.C.: Government Printing Office), June 1977, p. 8. This estimate includes the value of medical benefits; the CBO also provided an estimate with those benefits excluded, to be noted below.

[126]Timothy Smeeding, "The Economic Well-Being of Low-Income Households: Implications for Income Inequality and Poverty," in Marilyn Moon and Eugene Smolensky, eds., *Improving Measures of Economic Well-Being,* (New York: Academic Press) 1977, p. 180.

counts, although the "in-kind" arguments do raise important issues about public policy, they also greatly exaggerate the current well-being of the poor and distort our understanding of their needs.

Some of the arguments meant to demonstrate the "abolition of poverty" through the growth of in-kind income have bordered on the ludicrous. Edgar K. Browning's analysis, for example, depends on including the "potential additional earnings" of the poor as part of their income. This means that the non-working poor, including the aged, the ill, and single parents keeping house, are generally defined as being "voluntarily" unemployed, and the earnings they *might* make if they went to work are counted as part of their present income.[127]

Both that study and the more cautious one by the CBO, moreover, compute the supposed value of in-kind benefits to the poor by their market value (or by their full cost to the government). In reality, of course, the cost of providing a benefit may be considerably more than its possible cash value, even assuming that it can be assigned such a cash value. The problem with this approach is best illustrated by medical benefits, one of the most important in-kind benefits for the poor. Suppose that a family of four has an income of $5000 in earnings and cash transfers. Under the Census' definition, the family is poor, well under the appropriate 1979 poverty threshold of $7412. A family member then becomes ill and incurs $4000 worth of medical expenses covered by Medicaid. By the logic of this version of the CBO argument, the family now has an income equivalent to $9000 and is more than $1500 above the poverty line. As the CBO study duly pointed out, this approach "could count thousands of dollars in benefits as income available for alternative use . . . since the current poverty levels are based on normal health expenditures which may be small for the poor, this approach implies that a family can be made non-poor by virtue of large health costs."[128] Under the same rationale, a *really* serious illness could lift a poor family almost overnight into the ranks of the truly affluent.

This problem has been avoided in some studies—either, as in the CBO analysis, by also calculating the in-kind contribution without including medical benefits, or by calculating their worth as if they were insurance premiums subsidized by the government. Doing so greatly changes the context and the terms of the entire debate. In the CBO study, the addition of taxes and in-kind benefits other than medical reduced the poverty count from 13.5 percent of American households to 11.5 percent.[129] Measured

---

[127]On this point, see Timothy Smeeding, *The Trend Toward Equality in the Distribution of Net Income: A Re-examination of Data and Methodology,* Discussion Paper No. 70-77, Institute for Research on Poverty, (Madison, Wisc.: University of Wisconsin) December 1977, pp. 3-9. This study has a careful discussion of other difficulties in the Browning approach as well, and applies this to revising Browning's estimates (not discussed here) of changes in overall inequality in the distribution of income.

[128]Congressional Budget Office, *op. cit.,* p. 19.

[129]*Ibid,* p. 8. The study also notes that, under this definition, the effectiveness of transfers was much greater for multiple-person families than for single-person families.

in this way, in-kind benefits are shown to be significant, but hardly constitute a dramatic source of reduction in the poverty rate.

Defining the Poverty Threshold. Two other issues must be considered in evaluating the argument that in-kind benefits have substantially diminished poverty: the use of an inadequate poverty threshold to begin with, and the failure to consider the equivalent importance of the in-kind benefits received by the *non-poor*.

Critics have often argued that the official measure of poverty greatly understates its real incidence. That measure, originally developed by the Social Security Administration in the 1960's, calculates the poverty threshold by first estimating the market cost of a basic but minimal diet and then by multiplying that cost according to the proportion of the budget spent by the poor on food. Among several problems with that procedure, the key one has been that the food standards underlying the poverty thresholds are too low, since they are based on an emergency diet plan suitable only for short-term use; not on a set of nutritional standards adequate to maintain health over the long run.[130]

This not only underestimates the minimal cost of needed food, but, by extension, artificially lowers the estimate of the overall income needs of the poor. This often-noted bias helps explain why the Social Security Administration poverty threshold for a nonfarm family of four in 1979 was only 59 percent of the "lower living standard" estimated for the same family by the Bureau of Labor Statistics of the U.S. Department of Labor.[131]

A 1980 study of the cost of living for low-income people in New Jersey illustrates the inadequacy of the conventional poverty threshold. On the basis of an actual survey of current market prices for food, rental housing, and other necessities, the researchers calculated the average costs of a "Minimum Adequacy Budget" for various types of households within the state of New Jersey. This budget—which the researchers defined as "an unmistakably conservative estimate of a minimally adequate standard of living"— does not include any expenses for recreation, entertainment, reading materials, education, vacations, child-care services, food away from home, or other "non-essentials." For a four-person family, this most basic living standard would cost an average of $12,192 in New Jersey in 1980. The applicable Federal poverty threshold of $7450 amounted to only 61 percent of that budget. "The federally defined poverty-level income," the study concludes, "will not purchase those goods and services which the federal government defines as essential to the maintenance of adequate nutrition, housing, safety, and health."[132]

---

[130]On these issues, see the comprehensive discussion in Sharon M. Oster, Elizabeth E. Lake and Conchita Gene Oksman, *The Definition and Measurement of Poverty, Volume 1: A Review,* (Boulder, Colo.: Westview Press) 1978.

[131]$7412 and $12,585, respectively.

[132]Household budget survey conducted by the National Social Science and Law Project, pp. 14–16.

Another limitation on the adequacy of official definitions of poverty involves the way such poverty levels are adjusted to account for changes in the cost of living. Each year, official poverty thresholds are revised according to changes in the overall Consumer Price Index (CPI). But—as the chapter on Inflation and the Poor demonstrates—the cost of living has risen faster for the poor than changes in the CPI would indicate. This is because the cost of necessities (food, energy, housing, health care)—which take up a larger share of the budget for the poor than for anyone else—has risen faster than overall living costs. A poverty threshold based only on the *overall* cost of living therefore understates the real income needs and hardships of the disadvantaged.

When a more generous poverty threshold is used, the impact of in-kind benefits appears in a very different light. In a recent study, University of Wisconsin economist Marilyn Moon attempted to take into account both the value of in-kind benefits to the poor *and* the need for a more accurate measure of their needs. Moon's study focused on the reduction of poverty among the aged, using an expanded poverty threshold based on the Bureau of Labor Statistics' "lower living standard" and an expanded "economic welfare" measure that would include an adjustment for the value of in-kind benefits. When the two measures were combined, the poverty rate Moon found for the aged was only slightly below that estimated by the Census Bureau; more strikingly, the *reduction* in poverty among the aged was much *less* than it was using the official measure.[133]

Although Moon's study deals with the aged poor, the results are relevant for the non-aged as well, and are particularly compelling since the aged poor receive a disproportionate (in terms of their relative incidence in the population) share of in-kind transfers, particularly medical benefits. For the non-aged, it is likely that a similar exercise would show even less reduction in poverty rates, and quite probably a current rate of poverty higher than the official one.

Considering Benefits to the Non-Poor. Another key shortcoming of the argument that in-kind benefits have dramatically reduced poverty is the failure to consider the value of in-kind benefits received by people who are *not* poor. It is not only the poor who get part of their economic resources in forms other than cash. But the in-kind benefits of the non-poor—including health insurance, retirement plans and other fringe benefits wholly or partly subsidized by their employers—are not counted as part of their income.[134]

---

[133]Marilyn Moon, "The Incidence of Poverty Among the Aged," *Journal of Human Resources,* Volume XIV, No. 2, Spring 1979. This analysis covers the period from 1966 to 1971. Where the U.S. Bureau of the Census, using the Social Security Administration poverty threshold, found a little more than 30 percent of the aged in poverty in the latter year, Moon's measure estimates just over 27 percent; and where the official measure estimates a 23 percent drop in poverty among the aged over the five-year period, the decline was less than 7 percent according to Moon's estimate.

[134]For one estimate of how these affect the distribution of overall income, see *The Trend Toward Equality, op. cit.*

Clearly, if we do not add these benefits in assessing the well-being of the non-poor, we cannot reasonably include them in assessing the well-being of the poor without seriously distorting the measure of poverty used and the resulting comparisons.

Much the same is true for another issue raised by proponents of the myth of the "abolition of poverty": the "adjustment" for the underreporting of income. Studies that have gone to great lengths to calculate the precise amount of income that the poor fail to report to Census interviewers have generally overlooked the considerable underreporting of unearned income by the rich.

Failure to consider these sources of bias is sometimes defended on the ground that the non-cash benefits accruing to the non-poor are too difficult to measure. In part, this is true—especially if we go beyond the value of relatively tangible benefits (such as health insurance) to consider less tangible ones (such as the differential value to the affluent—versus the poor—of spending on highway construction or mass-transit facilities that mainly service the suburbs, of the value of various direct and indirect subsidies to homeowners).[135] But this reflects a political fact about the circumstances and situation of the poor, and cannot reasonably be used to support ostensibly technical judgments about their well-being. We are better able to measure the value of non-cash benefits to the poor primarily because we hold the poor—and the government—accountable for each and every penny spent. Yet we do not apply the same scrutiny and accountability to the often hidden spending of the more affluent.

This is not to suggest that the great growth in in-kind benefits since the 1960's has been unimportant, or that it has not significantly benefitted the poor. But it has benefitted them much less dramatically that the critics have argued—and in ways that are merely obscured if we insist on classifying these benefits as if they were cash income. In no sense has the rise in in-kind benefits "abolished" poverty, or even come close—even if we were to accept uncritically the existing poverty thresholds.

By even the most far-fetched arguments—like those that include the value of medical payments as income for the poor and thus enable them to miraculously escape poverty through illness—the level of poverty among some groups remains unacceptably high. This fact has been ignored by those who most stridently proclaim the "abolition of poverty," although it is clearly evident from the more serious studies on which their argument is based. Thus, the Congressional Budget Office estimate, with medical benefits included, left us with about 9 percent of American families with heads under 65 below the poverty level, as well as 16 percent of nonwhite families, and 12 percent of families in the South.[136] Likewise, using the

---

[135]For an attempt to unravel some of the problems in measuring "collective goods," see Burton A. Weisbrod, "Distributional Effects of Collective Goods," *Policy Analysis,* Vol. 5, No. 1, Winter 1979.

[136]Congressional Budget Office, *op. cit.,* pp. 11–13.

Wisconsin calculations, about 14 percent of people in female householder families, and over 30 percent of those in nonwhite female householder families, are still poor.[137]

Adjusting the Poverty Count to Include the Needs of the Poor. The picture is still less encouraging if, following Moon's analysis, we adjust the poverty count to include not only in-kind benefits, but an expanded estimate of the needs of the poor as well. Suppose, for exploratory purposes, we consider the proportion of people whose income is below 1.5 times the official poverty level. For a four-person family, this gives us a threshold of $9993 in 1978—considerably above the poverty level itself, but over $1500 less than the BLS lower budget ($11,546 in 1978). We then have a figure that matches the lower budget while accommodating up to $1500 worth of the cash value of in-kind benefits.

There are about 45 million Americans below this level, amounting to almost 21 percent of the population. They are 26 percent of all related children under 18 in families, and almost 50 percent of all people in female householder families. Two-thirds of related children in families with a female householder; over 45 percent of all people in black families; and 70 percent of people in black families with a female householder are below this level. An astonishing four-fifths of all related children in black female-householder families live in families with an income less than 1.5 times the Census poverty level.[138]

Again, these are rough figures. But they do show what begins to happen to the poverty count when we adopt what many consider to be a more adequate poverty threshold—even accounting for a substantial share of noncash benefits. And, even if we ignore the need for a more accurate poverty threshold, these figures very clearly make another point. They show how short is the distance travelled by most of those who have officially "escaped" poverty, especially through the expanded transfer system. This is strikingly clear for those groups most typical of the new face of poverty in the 1980's.

Thus, slightly over one-third of people in female-householder families are poor by the official measure; but about *one-half* remain below 1.5 times the poverty level. A little over one-half of the people in families with a black female householder are officially poor, a shocking figure in itself. But seven out of 10 still fall below 1.5 times the poverty level. Only about one-third of related children in those families are over the official poverty line; less than one in five lives in a family that comes close to meeting what one agency of the U.S. government terms a "lower standard of living." (Among children under six, the proportion is closer to *one in seven*.)[139]

---

[137]Danziger and Plotnick, *op. cit.*, p. 10.

[138]Calculated from *Characteristics of the Population, op. cit.*, pp. 36–37.

[139]*Ibid.*

Conclusion: The Outlook for the 80's

The myth-makers are wrong: Poverty has not been abolished—and there are no signs that it will be in the near future. It is not simply that some groups have not done as well as others, or that we have not gone far enough. The problem is deeper. Beneath the sometimes confusing mass of statistics is a discernible, and frightening, pattern—one that bodes ill for the future.

Growth in the private economy has largely ceased to "trickle down" to the poor in the form of jobs, better income, and a more rewarding and productive role in society. This is increasingly true, even in the South and rural areas where in earlier years economic development had the strongest impact on poverty rates. It is even more true in the inner cities where unbalanced national growth in the 1970's has simultaneously spawned a growing population of the "new" poor, heavily made up of female householders and their children, and even more disproportionately minority than in the past.

At present, all that keeps the new poor afloat is the income-transfer system. But it is misleading to exaggerate its success in reducing poverty, for even those whom it has brought over the official poverty lines are not far above them—and their opportunities for stable or rewarding work have not improved. However we evaluate the argument about the role of in-kind benefits their growth does not appreciably alter that situation, although it has helped mitigate the worst effects of economic deprivation. The kind of "growth" that largely characterized the 1970's brought us an enlarged population of the economically marginal, and has turned our central cities into something approaching welfare reservations.

Furthermore, all the evidence indicates that economic growth of the kind we have experienced in the recent past cannot, by itself, improve the existing picture very much. On the negative side, matters look worse, for the transfer system that has been the main bulwark against the ravages of the economy is presently under severe attack in an era of slower growth, increased military spending and tight budgets.

Based on recent evidence, the policy directions suggested by proponents of the myth of the "abolition of poverty" are desperately wrong and could bring tragic results. Their thrust is to de-emphasize social programs for the poor in favor of using public resources to stimulate the private economy. By all indicators, such a course would only deepen the crisis of poverty in the future. For it has been almost exclusively through social programs, and *not* through the normal operation of the private economy, that we have kept poverty rates from increasing even more severely in the 1970's. The trends of the past decade are very clear on this point. If we do not *expand* service and development programs for the poor—and for poverty-impacted areas—we will make little or no headway against poverty in the 1980's. If we cut back on those programs, we will have more poor in the 1980's than when the War on Poverty began.

This is not to say that overall growth has no place in the battle against poverty: Of course it does. Within the larger context of economic growth, however, we will need a new perspective for development—a kind of development that puts jobs and income for the poor at the beginning of our list of priorities, rather than making them the vaguely-hoped-for results of a "trickle-down" economic policy geared exclusively to the needs of the affluent. Without a· serious shift in our priorities, the myths of the 1970's—steeped in an unreal logic and buoyed by specious statistics—will establish the poor as the scapegoats and victims of the bleak realities of the 1980's.

INFLATION AND THE POOR[140]
(REVISION OF 1980 CHAPTER)

For the past three years this Council has been making two simple but very important points about the impact of inflation on the poor. First, we have argued—as have a growing number of economists—that Federal deficits have not been the cause of inflation in America as it is widely believed. Therefore, we believe that the assumption that spending on social programs is responsible for rising prices is incorrect. Secondly, we have argued that the concentration of inflation in the prices for the basic necessities—food, energy, housing, medical care—has resulted in a disproportionate impact on the poor.

Inflation and Government Spending

Unfortunately, there is little evidence to support the claim that government deficits are the cause of the inflation that has plagued the American economy for the past decade. To be sure, government can in theory cause inflation where it puts more money into the economy than it is taking out, resulting in "more money chasing fewer goods." But elementary economic theory tells us that this can only take place when the economy is operating at less than full capacity. Otherwise, an injection of public spending in the economy will generate more production and employment, often referred to as "priming the pump." It is only when production is already at capacity that new government spending spills over into inflation.

As the Council has pointed out, the economy for the past several years has been running with substantial unemployment and with excess industrial capacity. Investment in *new* capacity—spending on plant and equipment—as a percentage of GNP in 1979 and 1980 was at its highest level in 30 years.

Moreover, the fact is that the government sector as a whole has not been in deficit for most of the past 20 years. As the 1981 *Economic Report* of the President pointed out:

> If government budget deficits are the cause of inflation, it should make no difference whether the deficit occurs at the Federal, State, or local level. For example, the Federal revenue-sharing program, which grants Federal tax revenues to State and local governments,

---

[140]This chapter updates and revises a section of the *Twelfth Report* by the National Advisory Council on Economic Opportunity, Washington, D.C., 1980.

has the effect of reducing State and local deficits (or increasing their surpluses) by increasing the Federal deficit. If the program were eliminated, but both levels of government continued to tax the same amount and maintain the same level of services, the Federal deficit would be reduced—but the total deficit, and its inflationary consequences, would be unchanged. In fact, principally because the State and local governments accumulate funds to pay employee pension costs, their budgets usually show a surplus. . . . The combined budgets of Federal, State, and local governments have either showed a surplus or a very small deficit during the past two decades, except during recessions and for two years when Federal spending on the Vietnam war was at its peak.

The relationship between deficits and recessions is important to note. Our experience has been that Federal deficits have not occurred as a result of increases in spending at or close to full employment levels of the economy, but during periods of rising unemployment when unemployment compensation and other social welfare programs rise because of the increasing number of people out of work and needing help. In fact, OMB director David Stockman in his widely circulated "Dunkirk" memorandum to President-elect Reagan argued the same case. In pushing for the Kemp-Roth tax reduction program, he stated that the fear of deficits was overstated and that their major cause was rising unemployment which generated what he called "soup line" spending programs. Thus since deficits are generated during periods of rising unemployment— when the economy is at less than capacity—they cannot be inflationary.

Finally, there is the evidence from other industrialized economies. For example, both the Japanese and the West German economies have experienced relatively larger government deficits than the U.S. and have lower rates of inflation. In 1977–79 the public-sector deficit in the U.S. amounted to 0.1 percent of GNP compared with 2.7 percent for Germany and 4.8 percent for Japan. On the other hand, consumer prices during the same period rose 8.4 percent in the U.S., and 3.5 percent in Germany and 5.1 percent in Japan.

The Poor and the Basic Necessities

In the seven-year period from December 1972 through December 1979 the combined prices of the basic necessities of life—food, shelter, household energy (gas, electricity, fuel oil and gasoline) and medical care—rose at an average annual rate of 10.5 percent. While the overall Consumer Price Index for the same period was 8.8 percent, the 10.5 percent rise in the cost of basic necessities is a more realistic measure of the impact of inflation on poor families because the largest concentration of expenditures of poor families lies in these four areas.[141] In 1980 the gap between necessities and non-necessities

---

[141]Leslie Nulty, *Understanding the New Inflation: The Importance of the Basic Necessities*, (Washington, D.C.: The Exploratory Project for Economic Alternatives) 1977.

continued. The necessities rose 13.8 percent while non-necessities rose 12.4 percent.

The effects of inflation on the purchasing power of any sub-group depends on the composition of the household budget for that group, and the differing inflation rates of the goods and services that make up that budget.

The impact of the cost of necessities on low-income budgets is demonstrated in Table 6. The table shows that households in the lowest 10 percent of income distribution spend more than *119 percent* of after-tax income on food, shelter, energy and health care alone. Thus, many of the very poorest families *have to go into debt* to provide themselves with the basic necessities of life, quite apart from near-necessities, such as clothing, household goods and educational expenses. For households in the second 10 percent, 74 percent of after-tax income goes for basic necessities. Thus, households in the lowest 20 percent of income distribution spent 89 percent of their average after-tax income ($2054) on basic necessities in 1972–73.

TABLE 6
Expenditures on Basic Necessities by
Low-Income Households
1972/73

	Lowest 10% of U.S. Households	Second 10% of U.S. Households	Average Decile 1 and 2
Average Household Income	$ 1559	$ 3268	$ 2414
Less: personal taxes	$ 68	$ 130	$ 99
Average After-tax Household Income	$ 1491	$ 3138	$ 2315
Expenditures on:			
Food	$ 663	$ 943	$ 803
(As % after-tax income)	44%	30%	35%
Energy	$ 144	$ 187	$ 166
(As % after-tax income)	10%	6%	7%
Shelter[1]	$ 760	$ 891	$ 826
(As % after-tax income)	51%	28%	36%
Medical care	$ 213	$ 304	$ 259
(As % after-tax income)	14%	10%	11%
Total expenditures on necessities	$ 1780	$ 2325	$ 2054
(As % after-tax income)	119%	74%	89%

[1]Shelter figure differs from line item of that name in Bulletin 1992 in that payments on mortgage principal have been added in.

Source: U.S. Department of Labor Bureau of Labor Statistics, *Consumer Expenditure Survey: Integrated Diary and Interview Survey Data*, 1971–73, Bulletin 1992, (Washington, D.C.: U.S. Government Printing Office) 1978, Table 6, pp. 60–71.

When all prices are rising at roughly the same rate, as was true in 1970 and 1971, inflation affects everyone almost equally. If the price of food rises more rapidly than the price of other goods, a household that spends a larger share of its budget for food will be hurt more than one that spends a larger share of its total budget on other, less necessary, items.

Because the poor spend a larger share of their income on necessities than the overall population (89 percent for the poorest 20 percent of families, in contrast to 64 percent for all families included in the CPI), and because prices of all necessities have been rising rapidly, the broad picture is obvious: The especially high rates of inflation for necessities in the last few years have been more damaging to the poor. According to a government study, "Even small losses in purchasing power can result in major hardship for lower income households already on the margin of subsistence. Equal percentage losses in purchasing power across different income levels . . . result in a very unequal distribution of hardship."[142]

The Council also found that low-income households are much more limited than middle-income ones in their ability to shield themselves from the effects of inflation. Middle-income families can reduce their purchases of non-necessities and, to a certain extent, make substitutions or postpone purchases within the "necessities" portion of their budgets.

For example, although mortgage payments are fixed, people who own their own homes can delay maintenance or do more of the work themselves. Poor families, the majority of whom are renters, don't have a comparable option.

Regarding medical care, middle-income families can stretch the time between check-ups, and "many higher income persons can switch from specialist medical care to care from a general practitioner, from inpatient hospital care to outpatient care, or from private care to clinic care. . . . The poor . . . already purchasing the lowest cost goods and services available . . . have no such leeway and must bear the full brunt of increases in costs."[143]

The Council is distressed that the decision of the Federal government to decontrol oil prices and allow energy costs to rise will have its heaviest impact on the poor. A recent article is worth quoting at length:

> The option to conserve through reduction in energy use is not always open to those in the low-income deciles. Evidence published by the Washington Center for Metropolitan Studies suggests that only about 50 percent of low-income families own automobiles, and these are used mainly to travel to and from work. Opportunities to substitute other forms of transportation are usually not

---

[142]John L. Palmer and Michael C. Barth, *The Impacts of Inflation and Higher Unemployment: With Special Emphasis on the Low Income Population,* Technical Analysis Paper No. 2, (Washington, D.C.: Dept. of H.E.W., Office of Income Security Policy) October 1974, p. ii.

[143]Karen Davis, *The Impact of Inflation and Unemployment on Health Care of Low Income Families,* General Series Reprint 328 (Washington, D.C.: The Brookings Institution) 1978, p. 63.

available. Moreover, most of these families tend to drive old cars. They are also less likely to have the capital to purchase a more efficient auto.

The picture is not much brighter with respect to energy conservation within the home. The homes of the poor tend to be poorly constructed, poorly insulated and overcrowded. . . . Purchase of costly insulation materials needed to cut back on energy outlays is neither practical nor economical for them. The savings obtained by installing insulation take about a decade to be realized, and few sources exist from which loans can be obtained.

In comparison to the nonpoor, the poor own fewer nonessential items such as air conditioners, dishwashers, washers, and dryers. They can do little to cut back on energy, given the limited quantities of energy that they consume. The major determinants of energy expenditures for this group are space and water heating. Cutbacks in these are likely to have undesirable effects on both health and comfort. In short, the substitution possibilities for those with low incomes are limited. To the extent that price increases reduce the demand of low-income families for energy, these reductions are more likely to result from cutbacks in essential energy expenditures than from a reduction in other forms of consumption.[144]

Middle-income households can eliminate or reduce eating away from home, substitute cheaper cuts of meat and make fewer purchases of highly processed and prepackaged convenience foods. It is reasonable to assume that the poor are already buying the cheaper foods and so this option is virtually non-existent for them. A 1977 Department of Agriculture study found that a group of relatively high-priced foods rose 46 percent between 1972 and 1976, while a group of relatively low-priced foods, which poor households would be more likely to buy, rose 53 percent—a 15-percent greater rate.[145]

Other options that can help cope with inflation—drawing on savings, or borrowing—are closed to the poor.

The Council points out that when considering the average situation of the poor, it is important to remember that there are 25 million people classified as poor in the United States. Stories of people freezing or starving to death because they were forced to choose between food and heat, or of minor injuries turning into major medical problems because lack of money delayed treatment, represent some of the extremes of human suffering that inflation inflicts on low-income households.

---

[144]John L. Palmer, John E. Todd and Howard P. Tuckman, *The Distributional Impact of Higher Energy Prices: How Should the Federal Government Respond?*, General Series Reprint 331, (Washington, D.C.: The Brookings Institution) 1978, pp. 551-2.

[145]Alden Manchester and Linda Brown, "Do the Poor Pay More?" *National Food Situation*, June 1977, pp. 26-7.

Government Programs and Inflation

The primary response of government policy to the disastrous impact of inflation on poor families has been to attempt to cushion it in one way or another. The level of benefits in some of the income-maintenance programs has generally been raised to keep up with the cost of living, and several categorical programs have been created to subsidize each of the necessities for the poor.[146]

Social Security, Supplemental Security Income and other income maintenance programs are indexed to the Consumer Price Index, which has partially helped blunt the primary effects of inflation. This does not imply that existing benefit levels are adequate—only that they are responsive to inflationary trends. Further, the lag between rises in the cost of living, and adjustments in benefit levels and eligibility requirements, which occur only annually, means that very soon after an adjustment is given, the recipient's real income is already eroded by the continuing rise in inflation. The use of the CPI, rather than indexes pegged to the particular needs of the recipients, leads to benefit adjustments that do not accurately reflect the real change in the cost of living for recipient groups. While the CPI rose 13.3 percent in 1979, the cost of basic necessities rose 18.2 percent.

In addition, some significant programs are not indexed and are adjusted only at legislative discretion. In the Aid to Families with Dependent Children (AFDC) program, for example, benefit levels are determined by the states and most are not automatically adjusted for inflation. In addition, there are many states that do not provide the local share needed to qualify the Federal funding of certain programs for the basic necessities; thus, the poor do not have access to them.

The Food Stamp program is well indexed: Benefit levels are adjusted twice each year for increases in food costs (not the overall inflation rate). The various rent supplement and other housing assistance programs attempt to keep shelter costs to a fixed percentage (usually 25 percent) of household income, but they have never been adequately funded to help all who are eligible. Also, the CSA Emergency Energy Conservation program is not funded at a level to help all who need it.

Medicare and Medicaid have enabled the poor and elderly to obtain services that rising charges would otherwise have prevented them from receiving. There is no question, however, that inflation has adversely affected the overall cost of health care available to the poor. While costs have been increasing, the portion of their medical bills that recipients must pay themselves has also increased. As reimbursement schedules aree tightened as

---

[146]Executive Office of the President, Office of Management and Budget, *Automatic Cost-of-Living Increases in Federal Programs,* Technical Staff Paper, (Washington, D.C.: OMB) July 30, 1975; and William J. Lawrence and Stephen Leeds, *An Inventory of Federal Income Transfer Programs,* Fiscal Year 1977, (White Plains, N.Y.: The Institute for Socioeconomic Studies) 1978.

another means of restraining government costs for the program, recipients will be forced to pay a progressively larger portion of the cost out-of-pocket. The proposed cutbacks in Medicaid will mean that many of the poor will simply not get medical care.

It is critical to keep in mind that many of these programs do relatively little for the millions of people in families of the working poor—those who live in poverty or just above the poverty line. There are approximately 55 million Americans who are considered poor or "near poor."[147] In many cases, these near-poor families are the ones facing the greatest inflationary pressures.

The Council notes that more and more people with steady, full-time employment are forced to depend on such assistance as Food Stamps in order to make ends meet. This includes such categories of workers as state and local government employees and armed forces personnel.

Moreover, as Tables 7 and 8 show, there has been a substantial increase in the percentage of Federal expenditures for all human services programs while, contrary to popular rhetoric, the percentage of expenditures for human resource programs targeted for the poor has been reduced, *not increased,* since 1973.

Clearly, many programs designed to improve the lives of low-income families have become holding actions in the inflationary environment of the 1970's.

The new Administration's decision to seek substantial reductions and elimination of many of these programs will destroy what is left of the "safety net" under the poor.

Changes in Indexing

Over the past few years, the Consumer Price Index has come under attack for allegedly overstating the effect of price increases on the poor and the elderly.[148] Much of this criticism centers around the housing component of the CPI.

Because few of the poor or elderly are home buyers, it is said that the increase in interest rates and other home ownership costs should not be included in cost of living adjustments applied to income maintenance programs. Instead, all of the "weight" for the housing component in the Index should be represented by rents.

The Council agrees that the current CPI is not the perfect index upon

---

[147]*Money Income and Poverty Status of Families and Persons in the United States: 1976* (Advance Report) U.S. Department of Commerce, Bureau of the Census, Washington, D.C., Series P-70, No. 107, September 1977. The 40 million figure includes 25 million people whose incomes are below and 15 million with incomes no more than 25 percent above the official poverty level.

[148]*See* William Minarik, "A Critique"; Gar Alperovitz and Jeff Faux, "Missing the Point"; and Joseph Bowring, "Necessities Inflation and Distributional Impact," in *Challenge,* January/February 1981.

TABLE 7
Federal Expenditures on Human Resources as a Percentage of Total Budget Outlays, by Target Population, Fiscal Years 1961-76

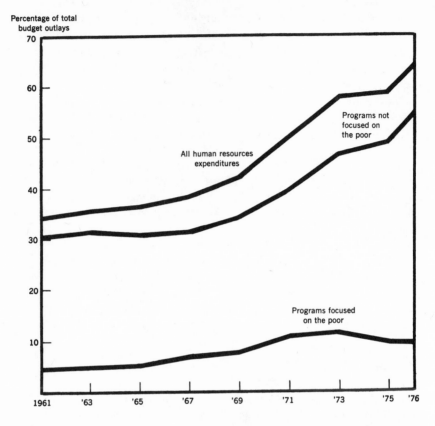

which to make adjustments in income maintenance programs and would support any reasonable effort to more truly reflect the increasing cost of living to the poor. Such an effort, however, must also consider that the most rapidly rising prices are concentrated in the basic necessities which the poor buy in greater proportion to their income. The Council supports the construction of a low-income family index based on a market basket reflecting what such families actually purchase. However, any effort to single out only those elements in the CPI which might overstate costs for the poor and ignore those elements which understate them is simply another cynical effort to reduce their income, which the Council unalterably opposes.

Inflation in the Basic Necessities

The history of price movements over the past decade shows a basic pattern: first a price "jolt," primarily coming from the energy and food

TABLE 8
Total Budget Outlays and Federal Expenditures on Human Resources, Fiscal Years 1961-76

	Fiscal year								
	1961	1963	1965	1967	1969	1971	1973	1975	1976
Total budget outlays ($ bil.)	97.5	111.3	118.4	158.2	184.5	211.4	247.1	326.1	366.6
Federal expenditures on human resources ($ bil.):									
Total	34.0	39.8	42.8	60.2	77.6	106.0	142.5	190.9	232.3
Programs for the poor	4.6	5.2	6.1	10.6	14.5	23.0	27.6	31.5	34.5
Other	29.4	34.7	36.7	49.5	63.1	83.0	114.9	159.4	197.8
Federal expenditures on human resources as a percentage of total budget outlays:									
Total	34.7	35.8	36.2	38.0	42.0	50.1	57.7	58.4	63.4
Programs for the poor	4.7	4.6	5.2	6.7	7.9	10.9	11.2	9.7	9.4
Other	30.1	31.2	31.0	31.3	34.2	39.3	46.5	48.9	54.0

Source: Henry J. Aaron, *Politics and the Professors: The Great Society in Perspective*, (Washington, D.C.: The Brookings Institution, 1978), tables 1-A1 and 1-A3. Because of rounding, detail may not add to totals.

sectors—such as the 1972 grain sale to the Soviet Union, the Arab oil boycott of 1973-74 with subsequent jolts of OPEC price increases, and the partially weather-induced jump in food prices of the past and current year.

The jolts then spread throughout the economy as businesses mark up energy costs and workers attempt to catch up to rising living costs with higher wages. Finally, misguided efforts to slow down economic growth result in high interest rates which are also passed on in the form of high prices.

Again, the result is disproportionate concentration of higher prices in the basic necessities.

Food. Food prices have been rising about 10 percent per year since 1972. The initial reaction when we see higher prices at the grocery store is to blame it on the farmers—but they only get three cents of every dollar that we spend on bread, and a similar small portion of the price of most foods.

There are three major causes for the food price inflation of the 1970's:

First, our food moves through a number of "channels" before it reaches the table. It goes from the farm to food processors to distributors to the grocery store and then home. Increasingly these distribution channels are dominated by just a few companies. Already 97 percent of chicken farming, 85 percent of citrus production, and over 90 percent of sugar production is controlled by companies which are vertically integrated (that is, they own not just one stage of the process, but each stage from the farm to the distributor). Because of increasing concentration in the food processing industry and in the distribution sector, after-tax profits in food marketing rose over twice as fast as food prices between 1970 and 1977.

Second, our agricultural system isn't protected from the shocks to the system that can be caused by sudden price rises due to shortage or bad weather at home or abroad. For example, after the Russian wheat deal, which resulted in large overseas grain sales in 1972 and 1973 (and also in large profits for grain speculators), basic food prices increased sharply, especially for grain and meat. The bad weather which characterized the summer of 1980 also resulted in the prices of grain and beef rising substantially. Because the U.S. is such an important supplier of food to other countries, we also feel upward pressure when there are overseas shortages.

A third reason for high food prices during the 1970's is the increasing cost of energy, especially for oil. Energy is used extensively in a number of stages of the food process, from the first stage at the farm when the farmer plants his crops to the movement of the food from the farm to the processor. Energy is also used extensively in processing. Transportation of the food to the store and its storage results in additional costs. Even farm inputs are heavily based on energy—much of the fertilizer and pesticides used in farming are based on petroleum and use large amounts of energy in their manufacture and application to the soil. As the cost of energy increased in the 1970's, so did the cost of these food inputs.

Energy. The principal reason for the increasing cost of oil and other energy products over time is our reliance on non-renewable energy resources. There is only a finite amount of energy in the ground, and the more we use, the more energy and money it takes to get the remaining energy out. It's like eating a bowl of spaghetti—the first forkful is easy but by the end of the bowl you're using more energy to get the spaghetti into your mouth than you're getting in return.

But our reliance on non-renewable energy only explains the long-run reason for increasing oil and gasoline prices. The actions of OPEC and the major oil companies have combined to drive prices up faster than they would have risen because of slowing non-renewable energy production.

OPEC set off the energy price spiral in late 1973 with its embargo on oil exports to the United States as a result of our support of Israel during the Seven Days War. As a result, energy prices in the United States increased 32 percent during 1974 and inflation climbed to unprecedented post-World War II rates of 11 percent per year. That initial large jolt to the economy was slowed only by a major recession which resulted in almost eight million people being out of work and the unemployment rate rising to 8.5 percent, the highest level in 30 years.

The embargo also caused U.S. policymakers to decide that the nation was overly dependent on foreign oil. To help encourage domestic production, we adopted an energy policy which decontrolled first natural gas prices and then the prices of domestic oil prices. As a result of decontrol, U.S. energy prices are climbing rapidly towards the artificially established OPEC world price.

The effects of decontrol, together with regular OPEC price increases, are enormous. It is estimated that decontrol will cost the average family $1100 per year during the 1980's while saving fewer barrels per day in imports than either strict enforcement of the 55-mile-per-hour speed limit or mandatory building conservation standards.

Now that the Federal support for speed limits and mandatory building conservation standards has been withdrawn, the demand for oil from upper-income groups will make the poor even worse off.

Housing. Speculation and high interest rates combined with a lack of planning by the public have resulted in housing prices going through the roof. Large numbers of American families are being priced out of the housing market, putting even more stress on the limited rental housing available.

The cost of housing is heavily influenced by the supply of old and new housing to meet the needs of an area's population. Because there was no program or policy which worked to anticipate the housing needs of the nation in the past and planned to meet those needs, we are now experiencing a shortage of new family housing. Because of the 1950's "Baby Boom," there are now a large number of people moving into the housing market. Changing family patterns with more single heads of household have also increased the demand for the available housing stock.

But new construction of housing is very sensitive to the interest rate. When interest rates are low, it is substantially cheaper to build houses and finance them than when interest rates are high. Yet the government, in an ill-chosen strategy of fighting inflation by slowing down the economy, has caused sharp drops in housing starts along with increased costs as a result of high interest rates. But high interest rates only make the problem of high housing costs worse instead of better.

In addition, the cost of land has been driven up over the decade by speculation and the increased demand for luxury housing. The trend in many of our nation's urban areas to conversion of existing apartments for condominiums has driven many of our poorest people from their homes as urban areas are once again becoming attractive areas to people with higher income levels.

Health Care. The United States has a health care system which is a loosely regulated collection of public and private institutions, insurance companies and doctors.

The cost of health care in the U.S. went up 117 percent between 1969 and 1979. A day in the hospital went from $50 to over $200. Unless a family has a health insurance plan, it runs the risk of going deep into debt anytime there is an illness in the family.

Many people place the blame for high hospital costs on labor—yet the share of the consumer's hospital charge that went to labor (excluding doctors) dropped 14 percent between 1955 and 1975. Meanwhile, the average doctor's salary in 1976 was $63,000 and rising.

Because of our system of third-party payments for health care through either insurance companies or through the Federal government, doctors have routinely been allowed to pass on the costs of expensive new equipment to consumers in the form of higher insurance rates. And the Federal Medicare and Medicaid programs have included almost no provisions which would ensure that the care which was provided to patients was either necessary or the least expensive available.

Our health care system has been heavily biased towards increasing technology, including more machines and more drugs, instead of minimizing the amount of medical care needed by improving the individual's health because there are no incentives or systems of cost controls which keep these high-cost approaches from being used.

Recommendations

The Council, for the reasons already mentioned, rejects the notion that cuts in Federal support for programs which serve the poor will reduce inflation. The Council also rejects the logic behind the present Administration's "supply-wide" tax proposals which postulate that the nation's economic capacity will increase productivity so rapidly as to bring down inflation. Nor does the Council believe the "expectations" theory that the Administration can convince Americans that inflation will halt and therefore they will act in such a way as to halt it.

The only way that people will believe that inflation will stop is if it stops. The first and most sensible step toward price stability is to freeze prices, wages and profits. *Therefore, the Council recommends the immediate imposition of across-the-board price-wage-and-profit controls.*

Food. To protect the low-income population from the huge continued and cruel increase in food prices, *the Council recommends the restoration of the full funding of the food stamp program per the previous Administration's budget request for fiscal year 1982.*

The Council further recommends that CSA and its grantees advocate legislation that would expand government (Federal, state and local) assistance for the establishment of farmers' markets and other forms of direct farmer-to-consumer marketing that reduce reliance on middlemen and provide less expensive, less heavily processed foods.

Because it could help the food budgets of participating households, *the Council also recommends the expansion of Federal technical and material assistance to help set up vegetable gardens in low-income urban neighborhoods.*

The Council recommends that the Director of CSA urge Community Action Agencies to become consumer advocates and participate in activities such as requesting supermarkets to stock more low-cost generic brands.

The Council further recommends that the President consider suspending import quotas, such as those on lean beef, that affect the price of food and other basic necessities the poor must buy.

Energy. *The Council recommends CSA experimental programs in utility-rate reforms be expanded to include the elimination of fuel adjustment clauses and the establishment of special rates that would enable the poor to buy small amounts of gas and electricity for essential uses at very low, stable prices.*

The Federal weatherization program, while not serving all who need it, has a beneficial impact on those it reaches. Further, because it is generally cheaper to save a barrel of oil by conservation than to produce it, the program contributes to national energy goals, as well as saving money for the poor. *Therefore, the Council recommends the continued development and expansion of the weatherization program.*

The Council recommends that consideration be given to an energy stamp program for gasoline, similar to the Food Stamp program. The program should include stamps for fuel oil, which has increased in cost more and faster than any other sources of home heat. The latter approach would also alleviate the especially heavy burden fuel costs place on elderly homeowners.

Because utility shut-offs cause immense suffering and a number of deaths each year, *the Council recommends that the Director of CSA urge State Economic Opportunity Offices to initiate and support state legislation that would prohibit winter shut-offs.*

The Council recommends that the Director of CSA carefully monitor the way the poor are affected by any energy policies that tend to raise the price of fuel.

Housing. Because the shortage of housing is the chief cause of inflation in this basic necessity, the Council opposes reduced funding for the construction of subsidized housing and urban homesteading programs. *The Council recommends that Congress expand subsidized housing and urban homesteading programs and place emphasis on the rehabilitation of existing housing in rural areas.*

Housing cooperatives can lower administrative costs and also reduce the amount of displacement in inner-city neighborhoods by allowing low-income tenants to buy the building in which they live. *Therefore, the Council recommends that Congress and the Secretary of HUD expand programs to increase the number of housing cooperatives for low-income families.*

Because it can help poor homeowners, especially the elderly, to maintain ownership of their homes, *the Council recommends that CSA—as the advocacy agency for the poor—urge SEOOs and CAAs to support property-tax reform as it relates to low- and fixed-income homeowners and oppose those property tax measures that are regressive.*

The Council also recommends that CSA give attention to those programs that will assure that rental unit repairs be made—and made on a timely basis.

The recommendations above are aimed at defending the poor against the immediate effects of inflation. Many merely seek to expand and improve existing programs. Others have been widely discussed in the past or introduced as legislation. Together they could have a significant impact on what the poor must pay for basic necessities.

Medical Care. *The Council recommends that the present Administration's plan to cut back on the Medicaid program be rescinded and full funding be restored.*

The Federal government has a program that subsidizes HMOs until they become self-supporting, but HMOs still cover only a small percentage of the population. *The Council recommends that Congress appropriate more funds for Health Maintenance Organizastions and specify that they be used to expand the number that operate in low-income and medically underserved areas.*

The Council also recommends that Congress increase its appropriations for nutrition education and other preventative health-care programs.

Finally, *the Council further recommends and declares its support for a comprehensive National Health Insurance program with universal application, containing stringent cost and quality-control provisions.*

THE HUMAN COST
OF UNEMPLOYMENT 1981[149]

For the past three years, the Council has gathered research on the social and personal impacts of unemployment—especially its impact on the disadvantaged. That research has consistently shown that unemployment (and under-employment as well) has a devastating effect on personal stability, family life and community well-being.

The Council feels that presenting this evidence is even more urgent in 1981. In the face of industrial decline, economic stagnation and crippling inflation, many voices in government, the universities and the press have called for policies to "shake out" the economy by cutting spending, tightening credit and other means. The same voices, at the same time, advocate reducing the income and job supports currently available to the unemployed—including Unemployment Insurance, Food Stamps, Public Service Employment and Trade Adjustment Assistance.

Behind these prescriptions is the argument that the forces of the private market will—in and of themselves—provide jobs and income for the disadvantaged. We have seen above, in "Poverty in America: Myths and Realities 1981," that this view fails to comprehend the realities of contemporary poverty. In addition, these precriptions call for massive economic "adjustments" whose impact will predictably be borne mainly by people of low and moderate income. This harsh fact has been masked, and justified, by the argument that unemployment no longer "hurts" much—mainly because of the "lavish" benefits government provides to the jobless.

But the Council's evidence shows, in growing detail, how wrong these comforting views are. Economic "slowdowns" in the name of fighting inflation; plant closings and regional decline ignored in the name of a beneficial market "re-allocation" of resources; cutbacks in public jobs in the name of (presumably) stimulating the private labor market—all these will have a drastic, and entirely predictable, impact on the lives of millions of Americans.

That impact will, again predictably, strike hardest at just those institutions that we claim to cherish the most—home, family, community, the ethic of work. It is a striking paradox that those who speak most insistently of the value of these institutions are often the same people whose preferred economic policies are most destructive of them.

---

[149]This chapter updates and revises a section of the *Eleventh* and *Twelfth Reports* by the National Advisory Council on Economic Opportunity, Washington, D.C., 1979 and 1980.

In the following pages, the Council again reviews and updates the best evidence on the human costs—in mental illness, crime, family disintegration and ill-health—of unemployment, in the belief that any reasonable and rational public discussion of economic policy alternatives must account for their documented costs as well as for their hoped-for benefits.

Is Unemployment Painless?

In 1936, a brief in support of New York state's unemployment insurance law before the U.S. Supreme Court argued that unemployment "breaks the morale of the worker, shatters family life, undermines physical well-being, delays entrance into marriage, depresses the birth rate, promotes sex irregularity, vagrancy, suicide, and crime."[150]

In the 1930's these beliefs were widely held, even by those who accepted unemployment as an inevitable, and ultimately even beneficial, feature of the economy. More recently, the idea that unemployment causes massive human suffering has been challenged, largely because of the supposedly ameliorative effects of social programs (such as unemployment insurance) that were created in response to the Depression. Some economists contend that since the 1970's there is a "new unemployment," cushioned by government benefits and increasingly made up of people for whom the lack of a job is a minor problem—particularly young people and women who are their families' second earners.[151] Indeed, some argue that government benefits are a major *cause* of unemployment, since—in this view—they diminish the "incentive to work." In 1977 the *Wall Street Journal* ran a series of up-beat portraits of unemployed workers living contented, leisurely lives on their unemployment or disability income. The author of a recent historical survey of unemployment in Western nations concluded that unemployment "can no longer be the mass material and psychological catastrophe it was during the Depression or at any other time."[152]

The concept of painless unemployment helps to justify public acceptance of recession as a necessary tool of public policy. Measures that would throw additional millions out of work become much more acceptable, especially when judged against the need to counter the devastating effects of inflation. At the same time, the idea that unemployment is thoroughly cushioned—indeed, *overly* cushioned—by government "handouts" helps justify cutting back benefits in the name of economic efficiency and fiscal soundness.

---

[150]"Social Wastage Due to Unemployment," Economic Brief in Support of the New York State Unemployment Insurance Law Before the U.S. Supreme Court, October 1936; reprinted in *U.S. Senate, Special Committee on Unemployment Problems, Readings in Unemployment,* (Washington D.C.: U.S. Government Printing Office) 1960, p. 180.

[151]Martin Feldstein, "The Economics of the New Unemployment," *The Public Interest,* Fall 1973.

[152]John A. Garraty, *Unemployment in History,* (New York: Harper and Row) 1978, p. 251.

After a thorough review of the evidence, the Council believes that these arguments are misleading and counterproductive. It is true that the impact of unemployment is no longer what it was in the 1930s. But the loss of a job is still extremely painful. There are few, if any, social and personal problems that are not aggravated by unemployment. Worse, unemployment creates a kind of chain reaction in the lives of the jobless, a cycle with profound consequences for the quality of life—not only for the unemployed, but for society as a whole.

Moreover, the evidence reviewed by the Council on the impact of unemployment on income, mental and physical well-being, crime, and family life, shows that the supposed "cost-effectiveness" of reducing benefits and other social services for the jobless is illusory.

Unemployment and Deprivation

The case for the relative painlessness of modern unemployment rests on the assumption that, because of the expansion of government benefits, unemployment no longer results in significant economic deprivation. But that assumption ignores the noneconomic losses that come with losing a job—the effect on the worker's self-esteem, hopes for the future and relations with others. In addition, by ignoring the limits on the scope and generosity of benefits available to the unemployed, the assumption greatly minimizes the very real economic deprivation many of them still face.

In September 1980, the average weekly unemployment benefit was $99.86. That was about $24 a week less than what full-time work at the minimum wage would have earned and over $40 a week below the Federal poverty line for a nonfarm family of four. In some states, moreover, average weekly benefits are considerably lower.[153]

More important, fewer than half of unemployed individuals collect unemployment benefits. Benefits are generally not available to people who leave their jobs, and not at all to those seeking to enter the work force or to workers in industries not covered by state or Federal programs.[154]

In a special survey in 1976 the U.S. Bureau of Labor Statistics (BLS) discovered that only 36 percent of their sample of the unemployed had income from unemployment insurance in the previous month. Even fewer (13 percent) had received Food Stamps, and fewer still (12 percent) had received public assistance. Five percent of the sample reported no income sources at all. The median family income for these workers was $450 a month; 14 percent reported a monthly *total* income from all sources of less than $200.[155]

---

[153]Economic Report of the President, January 1981, p. 273. In September 1980, the Federal minimum wage was $3.10 per hour; the poverty line for a nonfarm family of four was $7450 per year.

[154]Gary S. Fields, "Direct Labor Market Effects of Unemployment Insurance," *Industrial Relations*, February 1977.

[155]Carl Rosenfield, "Job Search of the Unemployed, May 1976," *Monthly Labor Review*, November 1977, pp. 42-43.

Recent studies based on a national sample of five thousand families show how serious the income losses from unemployment can still be. One study calculates that male family heads in the prime age range (35–64) who were unemployed at some point during 1976 lost an average of over $4000 in earnings. Even when unemployment benefits and foregone taxes were included, these men lost, on the average, about a fourth of their accustomed disposable income. This proportion, the study finds, has increased significantly since the late 1960's, mainly because of the longer average duration of joblessness in the recessionary mid-70's.[156] Another study calculated that 40 percent of families with an unemployed main earner in the 1975 recession suffered "serious" economic hardship; 25 percent suffered a loss of 30 percent or more of their income.[157]

These figures, moreover, mask the fact that many families manage to cushion income loss only by various coping strategies, from cutting into savings to putting more family members to work.

Studies of the Depression painted a grim picture of families cutting back on food, dropping insurance policies, exhausting savings accounts and living on what they could borrow friends and relatives.[158] Improved benefits have doubtless softened the severity of that pattern, but the overall pattern remains the same. The BLS 1976 survey found that seven out of 10 of their sample of unemployed were meeting living costs by cutting back on spending for food, clothing and transportation; more than one in 10 had been forced to move to cheaper housing; and 27 percent had been forced to borrow money.[159]

The loss of a job may start a vicious cycle, for it often makes it difficult to re-enter the work force. Many who lost a job in the "mini-recession" of the early 1970's began by cutting into savings, slicing normal expenses to the minimum and deferring all nonessential spending. As the time of unemployment lengthened, they used more drastic expedients: selling off insurance policies, moving into cheaper homes or apartments and ultimately selling cars and other belongings. Unfortunately, the loss of a car often compounds the problem because it interferes with the search for new work.

The array of government benefits actually or potentially available may make deprivation less severe than it was in the 1930's, but this can hardly be of much comfort to workers trying to subsist on benefits below the poverty level or forced to find cheaper housing. And, as the following sections demonstrate, continued economic deprivation is but one of many reasons why job loss remains a personally crippling experience.

[156]Martha S. Hill and Mary Corcoran, "Unemployment Among Family Men: A 10-Year Longitudinal Study," *Monthly Labor Review,* November 1979, p. 20.

[157]Phyllis Elkins Moen, *Family Impacts of the 1975 Recession,* Ph.D. Dissertation, University of Minnesota, 1978.

[158]E. W. Bakke, *The Unemployed Worker,* (New Haven: Yale University Press) 1940.

[159]Rosenfield, *op. cit.,* pp. 42–43.

[160]Katherine Briar, *The Effects of Unemployment on Workers and Their Families,* Dissertation, School of Social Welfare, University of California, Berkeley, 1976.

Personal Costs: A Note on the Evidence

The Council found that measuring the personal impact of unemployment is not simple, but that there are clear correlations beteen unemployment and a number of personal problems: ill health, psychological impairment, family stability, and crime.

Further, the official unemployment rate in the United States counts only those people who (1) are out of work *and* (2) report that they have sought work in the past 30 days. This excluded what the BLS calls "discouraged workers"—those wanting work but not looking for it during the past month—and even more who have dropped out of the labor force altogether.

Studies using the official rate seriously underestimate the actual impact of joblessness, while the few studies that take unofficial or "hidden" unemployment into account tend to reveal the stronger correlations between unemployment and severe personal problems. Even stronger correlations appear when *inadequate* employment—work in poorly-paid, unstable dead-end jobs, as well as unemployment itself—is considered.

The Psychological Impact

The link between job loss and psychological malaise—from general dissatisfaction to psychosis and suicide—is well established.

A striking effect of unemployment, consistently uncovered in studies since the Depression, is its crippling impact on self-respect. The impact is worse when the unemployed are forced to undergo a change in family status, that is, losing the role of breadwinner while another family member goes to work. It is worse, too, to the extent that work is defined as central to their view of themselves and their worth. A main source of the loss of self-respect is the tendency for the unemployed to blame themselves for their situation. Studies reveal that if they can "externalize" the cause of their unemployment, the loss of self-esteem is less: The higher local unemployment, for example, the less the negative impact of job loss on the respondents' self-esteem. The sense of worth is usually regained on becoming re-employed; but for those whose status in their family remains changed, the loss of self-respect is more enduring.[161]

Another study showed that the emotional impact of job loss is hardest on those in low-level jobs. Professionals and others in high-status jobs can often find other ways of putting their abilities to use after losing a job. But for people in more routine low-level work, emotional well-being is often wholly tied to being able to bring home a paycheck.[162] This theme consistently recurs

---

[161]Richard M. Cohn, *The Consequences of Unemployment on Evaluation of Self,* Doctoral Dissertation, Psychology, University of Michigan, 1977.

[162]Kay Lehman Schlozman and Sidney Verba, "The New Unemployment: Does It Hurt?," *Public Policy,* Summer 1978, p. 337.

in research on the impact of unemployment: The devastating emotional impact of joblessness strikes hardest at those with the fewest inner resources, the least ability to cope with it, and the least mobility.

Unemployment and Psychiatric Hospitals

Unemployment has a demonstrated effect on the incidence of depression and other forms of psychological impairment. One way of measuring the extent of severe mental illness is through measuring admission rates to psychiatric hospitals. As far back as 1935, a study of first admissions to state psychiatric facilities found that roughly two-thirds of state hospitals reported increased admissions in the first three years of the Depression.[163] More recent studies, using far more sophisticated methods, support the early conclusions. The most comprehensive study, covering the period 1852 to 1967, was designed to measure the impact of short-term fluctuations in the economy. Throughout the period, the rate of psychiatric hospitalization was closely associated with changes in the level of employment in manufacturing industries.[164]

A recent analysis prepared by the same researcher for the Joint Economic Committee of Congress examined mental-hospital admissions from the 1940's through the 1960's and calculated the precise increase that could be attributed to rising unemployment. It found that raising the official jobless rate by one percentage point could be expected to increase psychiatric admissions by 3.4 percent.[165]

An increase in psychiatric admissions may reflect factors other than an actual increase in mental illness. During periods of economic stress normal family and community resources for dealing with the mentally ill may break down or weaken under the impact of general economic crisis, thus forcing more of the burden of care onto public institutions. Likewise, a higher level of mental hospital admissions could simply mean increased hospital capacity—more hospital space for those with severe problems. One recent analysis that takes account of changing hospital capacities has reconfirmed that, for people of working age, the rate of admissions to mental hospitals is "decisively influenced by the extant level of economic distress."[166]

The Impact of Stress

Explanations for the link between unemployment and mental health have

[163]P. Komora and M. Clark, "Mental Disease in the Crisis," *Mental Hygiene,* Vol. 19, 1935.

[164]M. Harvey Brenner, *Mental Illness and the Economy,* (Cambridge, Mass.: Harvard University Press) 1973.

[165]M. Harvey Brenner, *Estimating the Social Costs of National Economic Policy,* U.S. Congress, Joint Economic Committee, 1976.

[166]James R. Marshall and Donna P. Funch, "Mental Illness and the Economy: A Critique and Partial Replication," *Journal of Health and Social Behavior,* Vol. 20, September 1979, p. 243.

focused on the concept of stress. Loss of a job is seen as one of many "life events" that can place enough extra stress on individuals to cause serious psychological damage.

Although the evidence is indirect, stress researchers have turned up consistent links betweeen the severity of "life stresses" and the incidence of clinical depression, anxiety and schizophrenia, as well as high scores on scales of general psychiatric symptoms.[167]

One study compared people who had faced few stressful events but had many psychiatric symptoms with those who had experienced much stress but seemed relatively unimpaired. The key factor was the degree of "social integration"—including the connection of stable employment.[168]

The same study points out that the steadily employed are able to buy the kinds of supports, including better mental health care and legal services, that can help them through a personal crisis. Similarly, a study of the origins of manic-depressive psychosis among working people finds it closely related to "role loss"—defined as "removal from the primary social positions and concomitant activities that one uses to organize one's place in the world." The loss of a job, if it cannot be replaced by another job or some alternative way of "organizing one's place in the world," can be the first link in a chain leading to psychosis.[169]

Other studies have shown that unemployment is not only a source of psychological stress in itself, but also a cause of other stresses that tend to weaken the individual's ability to cope with stressful situations. For example, unemployment is strongly associated with many other stressful life-crises, such as having to move or becoming separated or divorced, all of which are correlated with higher rates of mental illness.[170] The unemployed face not only the crisis itself, but also diminished finances to cope with it. Losing a job can set in motion a vicious cycle of other personal catastrophes that are much more difficult to handle for people who lack both the material and emotional resources that a decent, stable job provides. The impact on low-income families is most severe.

Women, Unemployment and Mental Health

Part of the myth of painless unemployment is the idea that unemployed

---

[167]Ramsey and Joan Liem, "Social Class and Mental Illness Reconsidered," *Journal of Health and Social Behavior,* June 1978.

[168]Jerome K. Myers, Jacob J. Lindenthal and Max P. Pepper, "Life Events, Social Integration and Psychiatric Symptomatology," *Journal of Health and Social Behavior,* December 1975, p. 426.

[169]Barry Glassner, C. V. Haldipur and James Dessauersmith, "Role Loss and Working-Class Manic Depression," *The Journal of Nervous and Mental Disease,* September 1979, p. 533.

[170]Ralph Catalano and C. David Dooley, "Economic Predictors of Depressed Mood and Stressful Life Events in a Metropolitan Community," *Journal of Health and Social Behavior,* September 1977, pp. 304-5. A more recent and comprehensive discussion of the impact of economic change on stress by the same authors contains an important treatment of some of the technical research issues in this area: David Dooley and Ralph Catalano, "Economic Change as a Cause of Behavioral Disorder," *Psychological Bulletin,* Vol. 87., No. 3, May 1980.

women suffer little because their work is often not financially "necessary." Recent research shows that this is misleading. Women who are confined to unpaid labor in the home suffer considerably more symptoms of mental illness than women who are employed outside. For example, women in the paid labor force are less likely to show symptoms of depression; and among women who do show such symptoms, those who work outside the home tend to be less seriously impaired than those who do not.[171]

Similarly, the constricting and isolating demands of the unemployed-housewife role, according to a recent study, may help explain the frequent finding that married women tend to have higher rates of mental illness than married men. In samples of various individuals, unemployed housewives showed the most symptoms of psychiatric disturbance and employed husbands the least. The measured amount of disturbance for employed housewives fell in between.[172]

Suicide

In addition to the strong links between psychological well-being and employment, powerful associations between unemployment and suicide have also been found. As one recent study notes, "Unemployment rates tend to be the most important and stable predictor of short- and long-term variations in suicide rates examined across time."[173] Research prepared for the Joint Economic Committee concluded that a rise in the unemployment rate of one percent would raise suicide rates by about 4 percent and that the 1.4 percentage point increase in the jobless rate in 1970 could be held responsible for roughly 1500 suicides across the country. According to the research, the suicide rate has been so closely tied to change in unemployment over a period of time that it is one of the more reliable indicators of the economy in the United States.[174]

Effects on Health

There is clear and persuasive evidence that unemployment affects health, in both the short term and the long. The researcher for the Joint Economic

---

[171]Jacquelyn M. Hall, National Institute of Mental Health, Testimony, U.S. Congress, Senate Hearings, *The Coming Decade*, February 1979, p. 678.

[172]Walter R. Gove and Michael R. Geerken, "The Effect of Children and Employment on the Mental Health of Married Men and Women," *Social Forces*, September 1977.

[173]Gideon Vigderhous and Gideon Fishman, "The Impact of Unemployment and Familial Integration on Changing Suicide Rates in the U.S.A., 1920–1969," *Social Psychiatry*, Vol. 13, 1978, p. 239. *See also,* Robert Mier, Thomas Vietroisz and Jean-Ellen Giblin, "Indicators of Labor Market Functioning and Urban Social Distress," in Gary Gappert and Harold M. Rose, eds., *The Social Economy of Cities,* (Beverly Hills: Sage Publication) 1975.

[174]M. Harvey Brenner, testimony, U.S. Congress, House Hearings, *Unemployment and Crime*, 1977, p. 29.

Committee calculated that there are clear links between rises in the official unemployment rate and the rate of deaths from severe illnesses. A one-percentage point increase in the national unemployment rate raises deaths from cardiovascular and renal diseases and cirrhosis of the liver by roughly two percent. This suggests that the 1.4 percent rise in the unemployment rate in 1970 was responsible for over 25,000 deaths from cardiovascular and kidney disease over the next five years. The rise in death rates from liver disease is directly traceable to increased alcohol consumption under the impact of economic crisis. Its effects on the death rate appear mainly within two years of the onset of a decline in employment.[175]

Researchers have linked the incidence of a high number of stressful events—including job loss—to increased risks of heart attack, chronic asthma, respiratory diseases, streptococcal infections, complications in pregnancy, and skin diseases.[176]

Long-term studies reveal that the loss of a job—and even the threat of unemployment—can have a striking impact on the physical health of the unemployed or threatened person.[177] But the effects of unemployment run even deeper, for they strike not only the jobless themselves but also, in one way or another, their children. The first and most drastic effect is increased infant mortality.

Infant Mortality

Progress against infant mortality in the United States has stagnated since the 1950's. Compared to other advanced industrial societies, the rate of infant deaths has worsened during the past 25 years. One study suggests that the erratic performance of the postwar American economy may explain that decline: Increased infant death rates have been associated with rises in unemployment rates since the 1920's. Deaths of infants less than a day old showed the most striking rise within a year of the economic downturn; deaths of older infants peaked three to five years later.

The study points out that fetal and early infant deaths are likely to be most affected by changes in the health of the mother following economic dislocation. Those changes are probably the result of drastic changes in nutrition, high levels of stress and hypertension, increased use of alcohol or sedatives, or increased smoking. Later infant deaths are more likely to stem from

---

[175]Brenner, *Estimating the Social Costs of National Economic Policy;* and *Unemployment and Crime,* p. 43.

[176]Ramsey and Joan Liem, *op. cit.,* and T. Holmes and M. Masuda, "Life Change and Illness Susceptibility," in Barbara and Bruce Dohrendwend, eds., *Stressful Life Events,* (New York: Wiley) 1974.

[177]Sidney Cobb, "Physiologic Changes in Men Whose Jobs Were Abolished," *Journal of Psychosomatic Research,* August 1974; Stanislav Kasl, Susan Gore and Sidney Cobb, "The Experience of Losing a Job: Reported Changes in Health, Symptoms and Illness Behavior," *Psychosomatic Medicine,* March–April 1975.

longer-acting environmental stresses directly affecting the child; lower income and decreased ability to provide or purchase adequate postnatal care lead to increased risk of accidents, infections and other preventable causes of infant death.[178]

Because they rely on the official unemployment rate, most studies may underestimate the effects of health on individuals without a job and their families. A study of the effects of job loss on "urban social distress" in 51 American cities used two distinct indices. One, the "exclusion index," counted not only the officially unemployed but also those not in the labor force but wanting work, as well as people working involuntarily part-time and those working full-time but earning less than adequate incomes. The other, an index of "inadequacy" of employment, included the same categories of people, but only if they were household heads and thus, presumably, most affected by being out of work or in a poor job. Both of these measures proved to be more closely correlated with rates of infant mortality and deaths due to pregnancy complications than the official rate alone.[179]

Unemployment and Crime

Researchers on the effects of unemployment on crime have found "general, if not uniform" support for a connection between high levels of joblessness and rising crime rates. The connection applies particularly to crimes against property, but usually for crimes of violence as well. In addition, the most rigorous studies tend to come up with the strongest links.[180]

In 1975 the Federal Bureau of Prisons reported that since the early 1950's the size of the Federal prison population had been directly related to the national unemployment rate. Increases in the unemployment rate were followed, after about 15 months, by increased admissions to Federal facilities. This relationship, of course, might result from stricter sentencing practices, rather than from increased crime rates. But a more recent study of Federal prison admissions found that the relationship between unemployment rates and prison admissions held true even when differences in sentencing were controlled.[181].

The Joint Economic Committee research estimated that one percentage point increase in the unemployment rate increased state prison admissions by about four percent. Similar patterns were found in Canada, England and

---

[178]M. Harvey Brenner, "Fetal, Infant, and Maternal Mortality During Periods of Economic Instability," *International Journal of Health Services,* Summer 1973. Patricia H. Ellison, "Neurology of Hard Times," *Clinical Pediatrics,* March 1977, p. 270.

[179]Mier, Vietorisz and Giblin, *op. cit.,* p. 376.

[180]Robert W. Gillespie, "Economic Factors in Crime and Delinquency: A Critical Review of the Empirical Evidence," in *Unemployment and Crime,* p. 602.

[181]*Correlation of Unemployment and Federal Prison Population,* (Washington, D.C.: U.S. Bureau of Prisons) March 1975; Matthew Yeager, "Unemployment and Imprisonment," *Journal of Criminal Law and Criminology,* Vol. 70, No. 4, 1979.

Wales, and Scotland.[182] These findings are backed by studies linking employment and/or labor-force participation rates with reported crime rates across a variety of jurisdictions: cities, census tracts within cities, states and the nation as a whole.

Further, a number of studies have found corresponding links between juvenile delinquency rates and reported rates of unemployment, and the homicide rate in 51 cities was significantly correlated with official unemployment rates.[183]

The most recent studies comparing unemployment and crime rates in individual states have reaffirmed the close relationship between high levels of joblessness and rates of serious crimes.[184] It has been calculated that if the unemployment rate in Michigan in 1975 (13.8 percent) had been reduced to four percent, an often-quoted level of "full employment," the rate of serious crimes in that state would have been reduced that year by 39 percent, or nearly 250,000.[185]

A 1977 study of national crime and unemployment rates estimated that a one-percentage-point increase in unemployment in 1970 accounted for 3.8 percent of all homicides, 5.7 percent of robberies, 2.8 percent of larcenies and 8.7 percent of narcotics arrests in that year.[186]

The study points out that the high correlation between unemployment and narcotics violations demonstrates how unemployment has a "compound interest" effect on crime rates. Unemployment leads to increased use of addicting drugs; the drug use, in turn, leads to much higher rates of property crime stemming from the high cost of maintaining the drug habit. Much the same "compounding" effect takes place with alcohol: Its consumption rises dramatically during economic crises, and the use of alcohol is, in turn, closely associated with serious crime—in this case, particularly with violent crime.[187]

Most of the recent research on jobs and crime reaffirms that it is not just the lack of *any* job, but the lack of a *good* job, that is most directly linked to personal pathology. According to a review of current studies on the labor market situation of offenders and ex-offenders, the strongest relationship between labor market performance and crime is "between employment stability (a measure of employment satisfaction) and crime . . . it is not so much individual unemployment per se which causes crime, but rather the failure to find relatively

---

[182]Brenner, *Estimating the Social Costs of National Economic Policy;* and "Effects of the Economy on Criminal Behavior and the Administration of Criminal Justice in the United States, Canada, England and Wales, and Scotland," *Economic Crises and Crime,* (Rome: United Nations Social Defense Research Institute) 1976.

[183]Belton M. Fleisher, *The Economics of Delinquency,* (Chicago: Quadrangle Books) 1966; and Mier, Vietorisz and Giblin, *op. cit.,* p. 376.

[184]William Nagel, "On Behalf of a Moratorium on Prison Construction," *Crime and Delinquency,* April 1977.

[185]Jack Nagel, testimony, in *Unemployment and Crime,* pp. 192–193.

[186]Brenner, testimony, *Unemployment and Crime,* p. 25.

[187]*Ibid.,* p. 44.

high wage satisfying employment." In other words, the broader question of economic "viability"—the quality and stability of the jobs—is more significant in understanding crime than is unemployment alone. Ex-addicts who are simply released without supports into the world of low-wage, dead-end, unstable jobs do poorly as measured by chances of re-arrest; those placed in intensive "supported work" programs that combine graduated rewards, close supervision, and serious training as well as a steady income, are less likely to be re-arrested.[188]

Effects on Family Life

Recent research confirms that "economic uncertainty brought on by unemployment and marginal employment is a principal reason that family relations deteriorate."[189] As usual, this effect strikes hardest at those groups least able to cope, materially or emotionally, with the strains of job loss. Thus, one study finds that serious marital dissatisfaction following the job loss of a breadwinner is much more common among the "economically marginal"—those with perennially low income and unstable jobs.[190] Unemployment also strikes most heavily at younger families, those with preschool children, disrupting family life at a time when stability is needed most. For children in school there is an adverse effect on grades and scholastic achievement and a delay in the whole process of child socialization. The impact is especially severe, too, for women who head families. They are much less likely to be able to cushion the blow by having other family members work, and collect unemployment benefits much less often. Only about one-fourth of women heading families during the 1975 recession, one study shows, collected benefits.[191]

Unemployment can also prevent families from developing. The absence of decent prospects for steady work can lead men to avoid the responsibilities of marriage and women to reject it. There are also a number of indications that putting off marriage because of poor job prospects or unemployment contributes to the high rates of children born out of wedlock among the poor.[192]

Again, a key finding in one study was that the factors often cited as mitigating the "new unemployment" made little or no difference in buffering the impact of unemployment on family life. Even those unemployed who were not the "main" wage earners in their families were twice as likely to report themselves as dissatisfied with family life as were employed main wage

---

[188]*See* Ann Dryden Witte, "Unemployment and Crime: Insights From Research On Individuals," in *Social Costs of Unemployment*, (Washington, D.C.: Joint Economic Committee of Congress) October 1979.

[189]Frank F. Furstenburg, "Work Experience and Family Life," in James O'Toole, ed., *Work and the Quality of Life*, (Cambridge, Mass.: MIT Press) 1974, p. 354.

[190]David B. Brinkerhoff and Lynn K. White, "Marital Satisfaction in an Economically Marginal Population," *Journal of Marriage and the Family*, May 1978.

[191]Moen, *op. cit.*

[192]Furstenburg, *op. cit.*, pp. 345-6.

earners. As in other studies, the tendency for unemployment to increase family tension was most sharp among those who had lost lower-status jobs. Predictably, too, family problems increased as the length of time off the job grew.[193]

Studies that have considered the effects of *inadequate* unemployment, rather than official unemployment alone, have come up with still stronger links between economic troubles and family problems, from divorce rates to rates of children born out of wedlock.[194]

Child Abuse

One of the most compelling indicators of family tension is child abuse, and studies consistently show that reported child abuse is much more prevalent among the unemployed and marginally employed. A study of stress levels and child abuse showed that, compared with a control group of nonabusers, the child abusers had more often faced what the research called a major "life crisis"—a series of stressful events coming one on top of the other. The researchers suggest that the precipitating role of unemployment in this series of events is crucial; in particular, geographic mobility and "the frequency with which families must be uprooted in order to find new employment" often lead to multiple crises in the lives of the child abusers.[195]

The Role of Social Supports

The destructive impact of the uprooting of families from communities points up a crucial finding in several recent studies; the importance of social supports in cushioning the impact of unemployment on the jobless and their families.

A study of displaced blue-collar workers from different job sites found that, since there were no differences between the groups in length of unemployment or the extent of economic deprivation, those who showed fewer adverse symptoms seemed to have higher levels of family and community support. On the other hand, those reporting less sense of social support were likely to report more symptoms of ill health, to blame themselves for their plight and to be more adversely affected by their unemployment.[196]

Unemployment represents the loss of one of the most important social ties—the connection to the workplace—that can help cushion the impact of personal crises. The effect is intensified if job loss and searching for new

---

[193]Schlozman and Verba, *op. cit.,* pp. 339–50.

[194]Mier, Vietorisz and Giblin, *op. cit.,* p. 376.

[195]Blair Justice and David F. Duncan, "Life Crisis as a Precursor to Child Abuse," *Public Health Reports,* March–April 1976, p. 114.

[196]Susan Gore, "The Effect of Social Support in Moderating the Health Consequences of Unemployment," *Journal of Health and Social Behavior,* June 1978.

work necessitates a change in residence or a break in ties with friends, relatives and the community. Even if the loss of a job does not force relocation, it involves the diminishing of social ties with friends and former associates: The unemployed may fear rejection, want to hide their lowered status or feel too humiliated by their loss of income and opportunities to maintain their personal relations with others.[197]

Again, the weakening of crucial networks of social support often accompanies *inadequate* employment as well as unemployment. Poor wages, for example, may force more members of a family to enter the paid labor force and/or increase their overall work-time, thus diminishing the time and energy available for mutual care and support. The result is both to make family members more vulnerable to stress, and to reduce the family's capacity to help cope with that stress. In turn, the weakening of the family's ability to deal with stress means that a greater burden falls on public agencies of treatment and support. This problem has increased significantly as inflation has reduced the standard of living of many American families—especially those with low or moderate incomes to begin with.[198]

Conclusion

The Council's research indicates that, despite programs to cushion it, unemployment remains an extremely traumatic and often crippling experience. It has costly consequences, not only for the unemployed but also for their families.

The changes in benefits available to the unemployed have not eliminated— although they have mitigated—the adverse impact of unemployment on economic well-being, mental and physical health, family stability and criminal behavior. Unemployment is still a potential catastrophe for individuals and families, and a source of expensive social disruptions for the country as a whole.

Economic stability is one of the most important means of achieving what is often called "primary prevention," or stalling social and personal pathology before it occurs.

The Council seriously questions the conventional wisdom that trade-offs between inflation and unemployment are merely issues of economic significance. Economists deal in quantitative theory, and behavioral scientists document the behavior of "deviants." After gathering the research of the social and human costs of unemployment, the Council finds it impossible to countenance the bland use of statistics and symbolic logic to mask human suffering.

---

[197]Briar, *op. cit.*, p. 53; Mirra Komarovsky, *The Unemployed Man and His Family* (New York: Octagon Books), 1973, pp. 120–130.

[198]On the potential impact of this weakening of the family as a source of care and support, *see* (among others) Urie Bronfenbrenner, "Families and Children - 1984," *Society*, May–June 1980; Elliott D. Sclar, "Community Economic Structure and Individual Well-Being: A Look Behind the Statistics," *International Journal of Health Services*, Vol. 10, No. 4, 1980.

The Council cannot merely accept the cost/benefit approach to human suffering when the consequences are unevenly distributed, bearing most heavily on those who can least afford them. Moreover, the Council questions the validity of using cost/benefit analysis without also considering the cost to society of mental illness, crime, drug addiction, child abuse, and divorce. Policymakers, economists and social management engineers seldom experience life first-hand in the real world of the poor.

Those who would consider accepting an economic slowdown as a way of controlling inflation must take into account the evidence that an economic slowdown not only increases the risk of personal crises of tragic proportions for large sections of the population, but also involves cutbacks in the agencies of social intervention and care that would lessen its impact.

It is crucial to the stability of our communities that the unemployed and their families have access to supportive social services, including family counseling, preventive health-care and nutrition programs, and other programs most likely to halt the degenerative spiral of personal crises with its ultimate costs to the country as a whole.

It has become increasingly fashionable to argue that slashing government expenditures on these services—and on income supports for the unemployed and underemployed—will boost the nation's economy and reduce inflation, all without serious hardships for the families and individuals affected. The evidence reviewed by the Council suggests that this is a tragic—and costly—illusion. Diminished benefits and sharply reduced services for the jobless can only multiply the disruptive consequences of unemployment—and ultimately require even higher public expenditures to contain, if not to treat, those consequences.

Historically, financial benefits to the unemployed have deliberately been kept low on the assumption that both unemployment insurance and welfare benefits may destroy the incentive to work. Unemployment benefits generally replace only about half of a worker's lost income. They are also available to only certain of the unemployed, and often, after lengthy unemployment, are made contingent on accepting work at lower status and pay. Many advocate that welfare benefits be kept low enough not to interfere with the incentive for work and that they be tied to requirements to seek employment.

But the preponderance of the evidence shows that most of the unemployed are willing to work, if the jobs are available.[199] And the value to society of using low benefits to enforce low-wage work is highly questionable, given the evidence that poorly paid, unstable employment is as responsible as unemployment, for the increased personal and family problems that result in increased costs for supportive services.

[199]Leonard Goodwin, *A Study of the Work Orientations of Welfare Recipients Participating in the Work Incentive Program,* (Washington, D.C.: The Brookings Institution) 1971; "The New Jersey Graduated Work Incentive Experiment: A Symposium," *Journal of Human Resources,* Spring 1974; for more recent evidence, *see* Washington State Department of Social and Health Services, *Proceedings of the 1978 Conference on the Seattle and Denver Income Maintenance Experiments,* Olympia, Washington, 1979.

Recommendations

Because of the intolerable burden on the physical and mental health of unemployed low-income families, the Council strongly recommends that the Congressional Budget Office initiate an annual impact study of the human and social costs of unemployment, inflation and the poverty that results, and issue a report on its findings.

Because it is extremely important that the media and the general public receive information regarding these facts, the Council recommends that CSA provide for the widest dissemination of the study.

The Council further recommends that the Committee on Human Resources of the Senate, and the Committee on Education and Labor of the House of Representatives, should give full consideration to the long-run cost/benefit aspects of these findings.

In the event of an economic slowdown, the Council recommends that the Director of CSA advocate, before Congress and among all Federal agencies, increased support for CSA programs and services to assist the unemployed.

The Council further recommends that the Administration and Congress ensure that any widespread economic dislocation be accompanied by increased services and programs for those most likely to be affected.

For the same reasons, the Council strongly recommends that existing programs for the unemployed and under-employed be maintained at adequate levels of funding.

The Council specifically recommends that the national "trigger" for state unemployment insurance benefits be retained; that Trade Adjustment Assistance (TAA) for workers whose jobs are lost through the impact of foreign competition be continued; and that Public Service Employment (PSE) through the Comprehensive Employment and Training Act (CETA) for the most disadvantaged be maintained and extended.

THE COMMUNITY SERVICES ADMINISTRATION

The Economic Opportunity Act of 1964

When Congress enacted the Economic Opportunity Act (EOA) in 1964 it declared:

> . . .The United States can achieve its full economic and social potential as a nation only if every individual has the opportunity to contribute to the full extent of his capabilities and to participate in the workings of our society. It is therefore the policy of the United States to eliminate the paradox of poverty in the midst of plenty in this nation by opening to everyone the opportunity for education and training, the opportunity to work, and the opportunity to live in decency and dignity. . . .[200]

The Act called forth a national commitment to achieve economic and equal opportunity for all citizens. It advanced three major goals: (1) to provide a broad range of new and innovative social services designed to enable the poor to raise their standards of living and to enter the economic mainstream, (2) to develop these programs in ways that would ensure the participation of the poor in policy decisions and in the actual delivery of services, and (3) to mobilize the private sector to cooperate with Federal, state and local governments in allocating community and national resources for the alleviation of poverty and the problems that accompany it. It also signified a clear recognition of the unwillingness or incapacity of the private sector and state and local governments to do the job, without Federal initiatives and standards and national policies and leadership.

The Economic Opportunity Act was designed to establish basic social service programs for the poor as well as to strengthen and make more responsive those programs in existence. In addition, the mandate called for comprehensive and accountable delivery of such services. It represented the most serious undertaking in this country's efforts to attack the problems of poverty.

The Economic Opportunity Act authorized a multi-faceted strategy that took into account both the causes and conditions of poverty in the United States. This resulted in the establishment of a broad range of human service programs, as well as local agencies to coordinate and administer them. The programs currently authorized by the Act include:

---

[200]42 USC 2701.

The Community Services Administration. In 1975 the Community Services Administration (CSA) replaced the Office of Economic Opportunity (OEO). CSA received the mandate to continue to coordinate Federal antipoverty efforts by: developing long-term national strategies; experimenting with new approaches; representing the poor by coordinating and evaluating existing programs; and funding Community Action Agencies (CAAs), Community Development Corporations (CDCs), State Economic Opportunity Offices (SEOOs) and certain other state and local antipoverty activities. CSA, which operates its programs through 10 Regional Offices, funds a network of grantees that operate programs to serve low-income families, individuals and targeted areas.

Community Action Agencies. The EOA authorized Community Action Agencies (CAAs) to: operate multi-service programs for the poor; mobilize resources for these programs; coordinate locally on behalf of the poor among public and private agencies; involve recipients in the planning and operation of programs that benefit them; provide coordination for the actual delivery of services of Federal, state and local programs; and ensure that programs would be realistic *and responsive* to those they serve.

The Council has observed that the vast majority of CAAs have successfully provided indispensable services and have won the respect and support of their local governments and the trust and participation of their constituents. The Council also noted that although 918 public and private CAAs now operate in many areas of the country, nearly 5 million—or 20 percent—of the nation's poor live in counties without them.

Community Development Corporations. Community Development Corporations (CDCs), utilizing private-sector techniques and management, are designed to revitalize economically depressed communities and neighborhoods. They were established to encourage business development and private investments, as well as to provide productive jobs in the private sector. They provide opportunities for residents to, ". . .through self-help and mobilization of the community-at-large, with appropriate Federal assistance, improve the quality of their economic and social participation in community life in such a way as to contribute to the elimination of poverty and the establishment of permanent economic and social benefits."[201] In the past several months two CDCs were able to achieve self-sufficiency, and CSA presently funds 37 CDCs that operate business and economic development ventures in rural and urban economically depressed communities.

The Council has long been a strong proponent of the community economic development approach and of the vital and critical role CDCs play in improving the economy of the economically depressed communities. The Council believes that this unique program is a singular example of private/ public sector cooperation and should be a model for further developmental efforts.

---

[201] 42 USC 2981.

State Economic Opportunity Offices. Because many resources needed in programs for the poor must be obtained at the state level, State Economic Opportunity Offices (SEOOs) were funded to represent the interests of the poor at the state level, advise the Governor and State Legislature on ways to attack poverty in the state, and provide training and technical assistance to CAAs and other grantees. The Council strongly supports this critical inter-governmental link.

Department of Health and Human Services EOA Programs

The Act also authorizes Head Start and Follow Through programs for the delivery of comprehensive health, educational, nutritional, social and other services to economically disadvantaged children and their families. Head Start and Follow Through programs are funded by the Department of Health and Human Services (HHS). The Council believes that these two programs have proven themselves to be eminently successful and necessary.

HHS is also authorized by the EOA to administer the Native American programs designed to promote the goal of economic and social self-sufficiency for American Indians, Hawaiian Natives and Alaskan Natives.

Innovative Programs

In addition to national programs, the EOA authorizes funding and overseeing a broad range of innovative programs designed and conducted at the local level to meet local needs. These include the development of trans-portation systems, rural water projects, fuel cooperatives, weatherization projects, housing assistance cooperatives, youth employment activities, family crisis centers and programs for ex-offenders.

Citizen Participation

Perhaps the most innovative feature of the EOA was that it specified that beneficiaries, along with other sectors of the local community, were to partic-ipate in the design, administration and operation of EOA programs. The Act specified that the poor or their elected representatives must be members of the boards of CAAs, CDCs and other local grantees that formulated policy, planned programs and allocated resources. Local programs were required to recruit low-income residents for staff and to develop paraprofessional and professional capabilities through in-house education programs, on-the-job training and a policy of promotion-from-within.

Based on the success of these practices, employing low-income residents and developing career ladders for them has become mandatory in many Federally funded programs. Many job holders in the private sector received their first employment and training in antipoverty agencies. The Council notes that this successful and important aspect of antipoverty programs has been often overlooked.

Economic Independence

The Council believes it important to re-emphasize a central point, that the primary objective of the EOA is to provide programs that are designed to end the economic dependence of the poor. The Council is concerned that, despite 15 years of experience, it is still not clearly perceived—by the media and even certain policymakers—that custodial care and educating the poor to survive at less than subsistence levels does not represent real progress toward the alleviation of poverty.

It is important that antipoverty programs consistently emphasize activities that encourage economic independence. The Advisory Council cautions those who administer the programs, both nationally and locally, to remain alert to the danger of a dependency concept in program goals and operations and to focus on the need for a conscientious rededication to the goal of self-sufficiency for the poverty sector. The Council believes that sub-human conditions dependent upon sub-standard "safety nets" are not solutions; but rather negative and illusory means of perpetuating the problems.

Representation for the Poor

The EOA provided visible and identifiable programs for the poor at all levels: the Community Services Administration (CSA) at the Federal level, the State Offices of Economic Opportunity (SEOOs), and local Community Action Agencies (CAAs) and Community Development Corporations (CDCs). It is the Council's observation that these agencies have served valuable and important functions as representatives of the poor and providers of constructive and productive programs. They have been instrumental in influencing the allocation of local, state and Federal resources to social and developmental programs that promote economic self-sufficiency for the poor.

While there may be differing views about the solution to the problems of poverty, this Council believes that this country must never return to its earlier apathy about the plight of the poor. Since the establishment of this Council its members—under five presidents—have repeatedly and steadfastly urged that there be a strong and effective Federal agency representing the poor. The Council still believes that the responsibility for representation on behalf of the needs of the poor still exists, and it must be done at the Federal level.

In recent years, as a result of policy changes and legislation a considerable amount of Federal revenues and social services programs have shifted to state and local governments. Programs affected by these shifts include General Revenue Sharing, Rural and Urban Community Development

Block Grants, State Health Services Planning, the Comprehensive Employment and Training Act, and Weatherization.

The Council has noted that administrators of such Federal programs tend to assume that local groups have the knowledge and expertise to plan a wide variety of programs in which they have little or no experience. These programs require expertise such as needs-assessment, planning and administration. These programs also require a degree of oversight on the part of state and local antipoverty agencies to assure that the needs of the poor are not being slighted by other interests. The Council's research demonstrates that without CAAs and CDCs at the local level, and SEOOs at the state level, there is little assurance that low-inc0me citizens will have a voice in the decisions affecting these programs and their funds. This need once again highlights the importance of CAAs, CDCs and SEOOs.

Therefore, this Council strongly recommends the continued Federal support of CAAs and CDCs and SEOOs. The Council is further convinced CSA must continue as an independent Federal agency and vigorously opposes the Administration's block grant plan. Historically, block grant and revenue sharing strategies have not reached the "truly needy." Moreover, they have created unnecessary local pressures and tensions by forcing programs to become intensely political.

Reauthorization of the Economic Opportunity Act

The authority for the Economic Opportunity Act of 1964, as amended, expires on September 30, 1981. In the past the Act has received a three-year reauthorization. The Council stresses the importance of Congress passing an extension of the Act before it officially expires.

A repetition of the uncertainties and other demoralizing factors that beset these programs just a few short years ago would be disruptive to all antipoverty programs and efforts throughout the country. Moreover, it would be a severe burden to low-income recipients.

The Council strongly recommends that the Congress enact and the President sign legislation extending the EOA programs for three additional years. CSA and the CAAs, CDCs and SEOOs are the backbone of Federal, state and local antipoverty efforts in our nation. It is absolutely imperative that they continue to function and provide basic human and social services.

LEGAL SERVICES

The Office of Management and Budget (OMB) has eliminated the $321.3 million 1981 Legal Services Corporation's budget from the Administration's block grant proposal for social welfare programs in 1982.

The Block Grant legislation, however, may allow states to spend the funds taken from other social programs for legal services support, a move which threatens to unravel one of the most successful social programs within the fabric of the justice system.

President Nixon, when he introduced legislation creating the Legal Services Corporation, stated:

> . . . legal assistance for the poor . . . is one of the most constructive ways to help them to help themselves. . . . [W]e have also learned that justice is served far better and differences are settled more rationally within the system than on the streets.

The lack of access to the legal system will be disastrous for the poor who may create problems for the rest of society if they lose one of their principal means of peacefully settling concerns within the system. A society that requires its citizens to live within the law must ensure them access to the institutions and remedies of the legal system regardless of economic circumstances.

The importance of legal services has not diminished since President Nixon introduced the Legal Services Corporation legislation in 1973. During the intervening years the Legal Services Corporation has been established and has succeeded in one of its principal goals—that of providing a minimal level of access to the legal system in every county of this country.

To withdraw legal services to the poor just as the Legal Services Corporation fulfills its promise of access throughout the nation is no way to convince the poor that "justice is served far better and differences are settled more rationally within the system than on the streets."

A brief history of federally funded legal services to the poor places current decisions in perspective.

The Initiation of Federally Funded Legal Services

A federally funded Legal Services Program was established in the Office of Economic Opportunity (OEO) in 1965. OEO and its successor agency, the Community Services Administration (CSA), operated the Legal Services Program until October 1975. Responsibility was transferred to the Legal

Services Corporation, created by Congress as a private nonprofit organization "after it became apparent in the late sixties and early seventies that a structural change was necessary to insulate legal assistance for the poor from partisan political pressures.[202]

The Corporation is governed by an 11-member board of directors appointed by the President with the advice and consent of the Senate. Under the terms of the Legal Services Act, the Corporation makes its requests for appropriations directly to Congress. However, the Office of Management and Budget may review and comment on these requests.[203]

The Corporation funds 323 Legal Services Programs which operate in 1450 neighborhood offices throughout the 50 states, the District of Columbia, Puerto Rico, and Virgin Islands and Micronesia. These offices are staffed with approximately 6218 attorneys and 2830 paralegal assistants.[204]

Minimum Access

In the Legal Services Corporation Act Congress stated that:

> . . . providing legal services to those who face an economic barrier to adequate legal counsel will serve best the ends of justice and assist in improving opportunities for low-income persons," adding that "for many of our citizens the availability of legal services has reaffirmed faith in our government of laws.[205]

When the Corporation began operations in October 1975, vast areas of the Midwest, South and Southwest had no Legal Services Programs. In many areas where programs existed, the minimal funding provided only a small fraction of the poor with legal help.

Consequently, the Legal Services Corporation immediately established a minimum-access plan to fund the equivalent of two lawyers per 10,000 poor people in every area of the country.[206]

Using this criterion, the Corporation found that in 1975 only nine million poor people lived in areas covered by programs functioning at the minimum-access level. Although another eight million poor lived in areas that had programs, these programs did not meet the minimum-access criteria. Nearly 12 million, or about 40 percent, of the nation's poor lived in areas devoid of Legal Services Programs.

Between 1975 and the present, considerable progress has been made toward providing minimum access to legal services for the poor.

Today all of the 25 million poor including 1.5 million Native Americans

---

[202]"Background," *Legal Services Corporation News,* October 1978, p. 1.

[203]42 USC 2996.

[204]Legal Services Corporation press release, February 1981.

[205]42 USC 2996.

[206]It is estimated that the ratio for the rest of the private sector is 14 lawyers to 10,000 people.

and migrant farmworkers have in their area a program funded by the Legal Services Corporation. Inflation has reduced the effectiveness of the Corporation's minimal level of funding, but no one can claim they are denied access by virtue of their place of residence.

All of these efforts to make promises of equal justice a reality should not be extinguished in the name of cutting waste from government.

The Nature of Legal Services Work

The Legal Services Corporation currently funds programs that in 1980 handled 1.5 million legal matters affecting the lives of millions of low-income people. Only about 15 percent involved litigation of any kind, and almost a third involved only counseling and advice. The single largest category of cases were family matters, followed in order by housing issues, income maintenance questions and consumer/finance problems.[207] Some of these problems were of major importance to thousands or millions of the poor. Only 0.2 percent of the total caseload, however, were class actions. The vast majority of cases affected only the individual clients of the Legal Services office. For them, assistance in many cases meant the difference between retaining and losing control over their lives, being able to remain employees and sinking into welfare dependency, seeing their rights enforced and feeling the anger and frustration of having promised rights denied.

To remove this tool from the poor in the name of budget cutting can only serve to alienate a critical portion of society.

State Funding of Legal Services

It is no answer to say that the states can fund legal services programs out of a health and social services block grant or out of their own funds. This is true even if some money is added to the block grant amount in the name of legal services.

Such an argument ignores the realities of state finances, the history of the creation of the Legal Services Corporation to insulate it from political interference, and the need for simplified, efficient and effective administration of one program rather than potentially 50 different ones with 50 different administrative bureaucracies.

The Block Grant Proposal

The level of legal services to the poor is likely to collapse under the weight of the Administration's proposed consolidated health and social service grant. The states which have traditionally shunned the role of legal services

---

[207]Statistics provided by the Legal Services Corporation Office of Public Affairs.

provider are not expected to draw on the grant, even if funds were included for legal services. Consequently, a race by varied social services providers for a share of the combined grant will obstruct the passage of legal services to the poor.

The Consolidated Block Grant. The Administration anticipates grouping approximately 40 health and social services grant projects into four programs administered by state governments conditioned on a minimum of Federal obligations. Financing for 1982 would reach 75 percent of 1981 levels, with the state determining which existing services would continue.

One of the four new programs would consolidate into a single grant a variety of categorical and block grant programs now administered by the Department of Health and Human Services, the Department of Education and the direct Federal grant program administered by the Community Services Administration.

Under this proposal, funds previously allocated for social services, child welfare services and foster care and adoption under Titles XX, IV-B and IV-E of the Social Security Act, developmental disabilities grants, rehabilitation services, the child abuse and runaway youth program, and community services programs would be combined and allocated to the states (at 75 percent of the 1981 levels) on the basis of some formula.

The Administration is probably referring to this program when they claim that states could use the proposed block grants to fund legal services. In earlier planning it was this block grant proposal that included legal services appropriations in arriving at the total proposed consolidated funding.

Except for very minimal reporting and auditing requirements, the only "condition" for receipt of the states' entitlement under the block grant would be that Federal funds must be used for health and social services. There will likely be no earmarking requirements, and therefore the funds will be available for one or more of the functional areas covered, at the states' discretion.

Thus, to fund legal services the states would have to channel some of the consolidated grant funds formerly allocated to one of the other services programs. In any event, the Legal Services Corporation would be abolished as a conduit for distributing Federal funds to providers of legal assistance.

Assuming that we have properly pinpointed the potential source for legal services funding identified by the Administration as available to the states, the total funding level for this consolidated grant would be approximately $3.75 billion, or 75 percent of the 1981 total funding level of $5 billion.

The Competition for Funds. Consolidation will not generate enough funding to allow state government to pay for legal services.

Based on current program consolidation information, the Federal assistance for these programs will collapse in 1982 by $1.25 billion.

The real effect of the reduction is more than 25 percent announced, since the Administration is proposing to fund the grant in 1982 at 75 percent of

19*81* funding levels. Due to inflation, the real reduction for 1982 is closer to 37 percent.

Moreover, the situation will be progressively worse in 1983 and 1984 when, according to the latest information, the Federal grant would stay constant.

The states surely will have considerable difficulty even maintaining adequate services in programs presently funded on a joint state/Federal basis. There is little chance that many states will *further* reduce the services under those programs in order to fund a *new* state program fueled previously by Federal funds.[208] Moreover, the substantial cutback in the programs to be consolidated into three *other* proposed block grants can only further strap state resources needed to fund new activities.

In the Title XX program, legal services have fallen victim in the wake of state financial stress. Title XX provides 75 percent Federal matching funds to the state for social services up to an established limit. The program allows but does not mandate dollars for legal assistance. Some states increased legal service funding before reaching their Title XX ceiling but the climb was tempered by competition for the funds from other providers.[209] Title XX appropriations are now being completely absorbed before scheduled cutbacks, sharply threatening existing service levels for other Title XX programs.

The competition between providers of services for funds coming from a single "capped" source will bind legal services organizations.

Title XX and the Older Americans Act (OAA), neither of which allocates specific funding levels to legal services, pitted legal services against their own clients and allied social welfare groups, and against state and local agency service providers who are able to use their special relationship with the sister agency administering the state Title XX or OAA funds to "outbid" legal services.[210]

Moreover, legal services will suffer because of the likely opposition to its funding from state and local agencies which are required to defend legal services suits from time to time. In a number of states, for example, suits against the state supported with program money (e.g., Corporation funds) have nearly cost legal services their Title XX funding.

In its proposed grant consolidation, the Administration has failed to

---

[208]Studies have shown that where new Federal money has been distributed without strings and for a multiplicity of purposes (e.g., revenue sharing), the effect has been that states use the new money to substitute for previously allocated state money. Apparently the Federal money does not stimulate expanded state activities. Surely it is fanciful to suggest that a reduction in Federal funds will stimulate new state spending.

[209]Since 1978, a number of legal services programs have lost Title XX funding, and in seven states that previously used Title XX to fund legal services, such funds are no longer available.

[210]The Older American Act, which provides Federal funding through state and local aging agencies for a variety of social services to the elderly, requires that "some" funds be used for legal services, but this is not quantified by regulation or administrative practice. The requirement, therefore, has had little effect on the scope of state discretion to choose between competing services.

acknowledge the "orphan" status of legal services in the eyes of the state. But for CSA, every project included in the combined grant—child welfare, social service delivery, mental health—is considered a state responsibility. Legal services are not, handicapping their efforts to compete for a share of the combined grant.

Federal categorical funding developed over the years to support these state efforts or to stimulate expansion of such efforts or closely related activities.

Indeed, the primary theory behind the block grant approach has been to *return* to the states the power which over the years had shifted to the Federal government as a result of increased Federal funding and parallel administrative intervention.

Civil legal services for the poor, on the other hand, have *never* been accepted as a responsibility by state and local government. It is therefore very likely that in most states the consolidated grant will *not* be used for legal services delivery.

Private charity and *pro bono* representation or bar association contribution marked the only significant legal aid funding before 1965.[211] There was a limited number of municipality-funded legal aid programs in the 1920s, but they disappeared when budgets were crippled by the Depression. By 1962 there were only five municipal legal aid bureaus (4 percent of the nationwide legal aid effort).

State and local contributions to the legal services effort remain miniscule. The Legal Services Corporation provides funds to almost all legal aid programs in the country. Only one-ninth of legal aid funds ($41.6 million) comes from sources other than the Corporation, and only 10 percent of those amounts are contributed (in the absence of Federal matching) by state and local governments ($4.4 million).

It is clear from experience with the Title XX and the Older Americans Act that states hold legal services in low regard. Approximately one-half of one percent of total Title XX funds ever reached legal services programs financed by the Corporation in 1981. That is $14.9 million Title XX dollars, 75 percent of which was forwarded by the Federal government. Only 17 states allocated any Title XX monies for legal services, and four states swallowed 85 percent of the total. Further, 10 states apparently ignored a statutory requirement to spend a portion of Older American Act funds on legal services and earmarked nothing for legal programs.[212]

Even if some states *were* to use consolidated grant funds or new state monies for legal aid to the poor, those funds would likely be channeled to criminal representation, where state and local responsibility is constitutionally mandated despite inadequate funding.

---

[211]By 1960, legal aid was 60 percent community chest, 15 percent bar, 25 percent special campaigns and *pro bono*.

[212]While the situation was worse before this limited earmarking requirement was added to the Act, the overall commitment to legal services remains weak. This is evidenced by the very small amounts devoted by some agencies to legal services in order to be in technical compliance with the Act.

Independence from Government

Importantly, the Legal Services Corporation is independent, free from the managerial labors of government officials. Its budget and policy are nevertheless established by Congress. To relinquish administration of legal services to the states would be to place their attorneys in the crossfire of political tensions generated at the state level, destroying the program's carefully drawn independence and scarring the attorney-client relationship.

Under the Canons of Ethics, attorneys owe complete loyalty to their client, and are especially cautioned not to be deflected from the clients' interest even if compensation is paid by another. Such loyalties are tested when the clients' needs are opposed not only by influential members of the community, but by the government source of the attorneys' income as well.

In light of these tensions, one of the greatest strengths of the legal services program is that its attorneys have not avoided their responsibility to challenge Federal, state and local laws and regulations, commercial business practices, and the procedural rules of the judicial system itself when necessary to protect the legal rights of their clients.

Advocacy of client interests before the courts and before regulatory and legislative bodies has resolved significant economic, social and family problems that otherwise may not have been addressed by the appropriate government officials. Housing, welfare, landlord-tenant, domestic relations and consumer laws and practices have been subjected to judicial, administrative and legislative scrutiny, and modified as a result.

The controversial nature of this sort of client advocacy, however unremarkable it is when conducted by private attorneys on behalf of paying clients, caused many governmental bodies and business interests to seek the elimination of legal services funding, or the imposition of severe restrictions on the scope of representational activities, when the program was funded under the Economic Opportunity Act. At that time, governors were able to veto prospective legal services grants in their states (subject to the OEO Director's override). As a consequence of successful legal services litigation against state and local governments or powerful commercial interests, program grants in at least six states were vetoed (California, Florida, Missouri, Connecticut, Louisiana and North Dakota), and others were threatened. A veto threat kept South Carolina without legal services for the poor for six years.

The threat of political interference with legal services delivery did not originate with the OEO program. Mayors with government-supported legal aid services withdrew funds early on when programs failed to respond to political demands. Merchants, landlords and others pressured privately funded legal aid operations to refuse such cases as bankruptcy. A book published by the Russel Sage Foundation reported in 1966 that there was a "tendency . . . for legal aid to become a captive of its principal financial supporters."

In the late 1960s and early 1970s, in the wake of political interference, the question of the appropriate location of the legal services program received the attention of the organized bar, the Executive Branch and the Congress.

Alternatives to OEO, such as housing the program in a Cabinet-level agency such as HEW, HUD or the Department of Justice, or in state or local government, were considered.

Every major group to consider the matter, including the American Bar Association (ABA), President Nixon's Advisory Council on Executive Organization (Ash Commission) and the National Advisory Committee on the Legal Services Program, concluded that a private corporation, *independent from government*, should be established to insure the program's integrity, survival and effectiveness.[213]

The ABA found that locating the program in a Cabinet agency would create a conflict of interest in light of the numerous legal services suits against these agencies, and the Federal agencies' close-working relationship with state and local governments, who were also frequently parties to legal services litigation. The Justice possibility was considered especially vulnerable since its lawyers were responsible for defending legal services suits against Federal government.

Moreover, apart from the appearance of a conflict of interest in particular suits, the ABA viewed as untenable the competition for scarce budget resources that would be waged within the Department of Justice between legal services and government lawyer operations. The Ash Commission observed that:

> subordination of this program within a line department, would . . . place within the Departments, a program funding lawyers whose caseload would at times involve suits against agencies within the same department. This we view as a conflict of interest that would inhibit the proper functioning of the program.

And the National Advisory Committee informed the President as follows:

> The integrity of the lawyer-client relationship must be preserved free of interference by outside sources. Particularly, this means freedom from political pressure and conflicting governmental policies which detract from the lawyer's duty of absolute fidelity to his client. This can probably best be attained by establishing a structure *independent of any federal, state or local governmental department or agency.* [Emphasis added.]

President Nixon agreed. In his message to Congress proposing the new Legal Services Corporation, the President noted that "much of the litigation initiated by legal services has placed it in direct conflict with local and state governments. The program is concerned with social issues and is thus subject

---

[213]The National Advisory Committee consisted of Attorney General Mitchell, HEW Secretary Richardson, past, current and future ABA presidents, law school deans and professors, private practitioners, businessmen, private citizens and legal aid attorneys.

to unusually strong political pressures." The President urged that a corporation be structured and financed to assure the program of the independence it needed and to provide legal services attorneys the "full freedom to protect the best interests of their clients in keeping with the Canons of Ethics and the high standards of the legal profession."

The Congress accepted the unanimous recommendations and followed the President's lead. It declared in the first section of the legal Services Corporation Act that "the legal services program must be kept free from the influence of or use by it of political pressures."[214]

To accomplish this purpose, Congress created a structure that assures independence from political interference and conflicts of interest. The Board of the Corporation, not an official of the Executive Branch, sets general policy and funding priorities, and its members are removable only for cause. Political qualifications may not be used as a test for employee hiring, political activity by Corporation or recipient employees is barred, and the Corporation may not undertake to represent clients other than itself.

Moreover, in recognition that grants to state and local governments would undercut this structural independence, Congress has limited the Corporation's authority to fund state and local governments to situations where it is demonstrated that non-governmental agencies are unable to adequately deliver the needed services.[215]

If the states manage legal services to the poor as ordered in the President's budget, they will not be able to meet many fundamental client needs. A conflict of interest is inevitable, for example, if the state assigns legal services programs to the welfare department or Attorney General's Office. Legal services would be vulnerable to pressure from other agencies challenged by legal services, their funding decisions open to controversy. States' action under Title XX, the Older Americans Act and other limited legal services programs fueled by Federal grants bears testimony to such interference. Legal services programs in certain states cannot use state funds to sue the state or its agencies. Others are barred from funds to challenge administrative procedures or prevented from using class actions despite its benefit to clients. Prior notice of litigation against the state has also been required. States have wielded funding cutoffs, extraordinary grant conditions or detailed audits against Title XX programs taking the state to court.[216]

---

[214]Section 1001(5).

[215]It is interesting to note that no state government has ever requested LSC funding for legal services, demonstrating either their lack of interest or the adequacy of the current programs, or both.

[216]Because of the changing needs of other service providers who compete for a piece of the same pie, and the changing preferences of non-lawyer government officials who are not sympathetic to or understanding of the needs of legal services, funding for legal services under the various grant programs has been uncertain from year to year. As a result, many legal services programs perceive an indirect pressure to avoid controversial litigation in order to be able to compete successfully for future grants. This effect would be greater if Corporation funding for the bulk of program operations were withdrawn.

In sum, shifting responsibility for legal services from an independent corporation to state government would reverse the significant progress made during the last decade by Republican and Democratic Administrations and members of Congress to insulate the delivery of legal services from political pressure and manipulation.

The Current Program vs. State Operation

The existing legal services program already accomplishes goals set forth by the Administration in consolidation: local control, reduction of Federal regulation and streamlined program operation. Transferring responsibility to the state is unnecessary and may prove seriously damaging.

There are very few Federally mandated categorical restrictions on legal services grants. Recipients set their own priorities within the very broad program goals established by Congress, for example, to promote equal access to justice (§1001(1)), and to deliver an effective service in an economical fashion (§1007(a)(3)).

This enormous flexibility built into the enabling statute has in fact led to significant diversity in the types of programs funded throughout the country.

Some programs serve small geographic areas, others entire states; some are located in sparsely populated rural areas, others in dense urban areas; some rely entirely on full-time staff attorneys, others rely heavily on *pro bono* participation by the private bar, and still others utilize a paid private lawyer model under which private practitioners are under contract or are reimbursed on a case-by-case basis. Where necessary, some programs have developed special units to serve particular client groups in their community (such as the elderly, handicapped, Native Americans or migrant workers) who might otherwise be underserved or who have unique legal needs requiring special attention.

The legal services program now in place distinctly addresses the Administration's proposal to focus the block grant on the community.

The Legal Services Corporation Act provides for control and supervision of the operation of legal services programs by local community leaders, as well as local political input into funding decisions by the Corporation. Each of the 323 separate local programs (including more than 1400 offices in every county of the country) is required to be run by a board of directors, 60 percent of whom must be members of the local bar and one-third eligible clients from the community served.

It is the local board that sets work priorities, establishes evaluation and case review mechanisms to assure that clients receive the quality representation to which they are entitled, determines the need for and site locations for branch offices, and decides how to obtain private bar assistance in meeting community legal needs.

The existing program also solicits the views of state and local officials. Under the Act, each governor appoints a State Advisory Council, comprised of local attorneys recommended by the state bar, to advise the Corporation of possible violations of the Act by grantees in the state.

In addition, to assure that elected local officials and the local bar have an opportunity to educate Corporation officials about the needs in their communities and the wisdom of particular funding decisions, the Act provides for prior notice to the Governor and local bar of a proposed grant, together with a request for comments.

This furthers local participation without the danger of political pressure and control fostered by the veto power under the Economic Opportunity Act.

There is no interference with local autonomy in the management of legal services apart from reasonable fiscal controls, and the Act itself encourages or requires effective community participation in the programs.

Consolidation of grant services under the umbrella of state government, should it choose to recognize legal services, will duplicate and balloon administrative costs and insert a new chapter of bureaucracy between recipients and Federal funding sources. The Legal Services Corporation has maintained a minimal, three-percent operating tab, and registered significant savings in technical advocacy assistance to the poor, national training and additional support activities. These would be erased.

Also endangered are established information-sharing systems distributed through a poverty law journal to all local programs along with specialized support project funding. Individually, states would be financially hamstrung to reproduce these efforts.

The elimination of the Corporation as a centralized agency for administering the program would not increase administrative costs solely by virtue of its effect on duplication of resources. The absence of targeted funding for legal services makes it likely that any legal services funding provided by the states would be operated as part of a larger bureaucracy whose mission is devoted to the delivery of other services unlike legal services.

Administration by persons who have little knowledge about legal services would minimize the role of those most familiar with the legal needs of the community (i.e., the local bar and the clients), and can be expected to result in costly and unnecessary administrative requirements that limit the effectiveness of the funds provided.

As *The New York Times* maintained in an editorial, Sunday, March 8, 1981: "[T]o kill the program, under the pretense that the states are free to keep it alive, is unconscionable. The issue is not whether to save money; it is whether to preserve justice."

Recommendation

Consistent with the principle of providing equal access to justice, the Council unanimously supports an independent Legal Services Corporation and recommends passage of HR3480 at full authorization.

AMERICAN VALUES, CITIZENSHIP
AND THE POLITICAL ECONOMY:[217]
PROSPECT FOR THE 80's

The Dilemma

As the decade of the 70's came to a close it became clear that a substantial majority of Americans believed our society to be serious trouble. For the first time in our history most Americans think their future will be worse, not better, than their past. For the first time in our history most Americans think their children's prospects are worse, not better, than their own.

Though this new pessimism has many sources, the most prominent cause is certainly anxiety about the economy. Public opinion surveys indicate that economic issues are dominating public consciousness. There is concern about recession and unemployment, particularly of youth and minorities. There is concern about energy. But above all there is genuine fear over unchecked inflation. Inflation undermines security about the future, creates doubt and suspicion of our fellow citizens and undercuts the commitments that make democracy possible.

In these conditions the economic sector becomes a microcosm of the whole society. Doubts and anxieties about our institutions that have been fed by the Vietnam War and the Watergate scandal are deepened by our apparent inability to deal with severe economic difficulties. The "moral malaise" to which President Carter pointed in 1980 is perhaps more evident in our economic institutions than anywhere else in our public life.

Moreover, in our present state of economic uncertainty there has been a tendency for public action to degenerate into the narrowest pursuit of private interest. The more affluent seek to ease the strain by redistributing income from the poor to themselves through such devices as California's Proposition 13, and a range of similar initiatives in other states. Economic stringency and rising rates of unemployment for those below the median income are defended as "acceptable costs" that will among other things "improve labor discipline." There are those who would use our present economic troubles to institutionalize a kind of socio-economic triage.

Meanwhile, 25 million Americans are poor and another 30 million are near poor, so that one-third of our citizens are materially deprived. Those least

---

[217]This chapter updates and revises a section of the *Twelfth Report* by the National Advisory Council on Economic Opportunity, Washington, D.C., 1980.

able to defend themselves economically suffer the most from inflation. The cost is high not only in material deprivation but also in political withdrawal, for poverty is not a condition for effective citizenship.

The historian Sam Bass Warner, Jr., writes that we are on "the eve of the collapse of the national private economy."[218] The Chrysler Corporation may be only the tip of the iceberg. The economic forecasts of the *Wall Street Journal* are bleak. Indeed, much of the private economy survives only because of direct or indirect subsidization (contracts, tariffs, protectionist trade agreements and tax benefits) by the Federal government, that most ironic form of "welfare."

Under these conditions the Council must ask not only what can be done to solve the present problem of poverty, but what can be done to keep poverty from engulfing the nation. How, for example, do we control inflation? Yet the Council also recognizes that the answers to these problems cannot be purely economic and technical. The economy is a central sector of our social fabric, closely bound up with all our other institutions. It is not working very well and it is working much less well for some than for others. Thus the Council must also ask what kind of social and political problems does the economy give rise to, and how can these be dealt with.

In addition, the Council must pose the question, how can America, in the economic arena, enhance democratic citizenship and avoid the drift to authoritarianism? We believe that the best way to begin to seek answers to these crucial problems is to look at our present in the context of our past, to seriously consider the history of our nation and seek out what the American democratic tradition has to say about economic institutions and how that tradition can be adapted to our present needs.

The Economy in a Democracy

In *Democracy in America*, perhaps the wisest book ever written about America, Alexis de Tocqueville argued 150 years ago that though the physical circumstances of our country contribute to our public happiness, the laws contribute more than the physical circumstances, and the mores more than the laws. We were fortunate indeed to inherit from the founders of our republic a constitutional and legal order that has proven sound and flexible. But the origin, interpretation and perpetuation of that order are dependent on the mores embedded in society. A society with different mores would long since have eroded and subverted our constitutional and legal order. De Tocqueville defines "mores" as "habits of the heart," "the sum of moral and intellectual dispositions of men in society."[219] The mores include the

---

[218]Sam Bass Warner, Jr., *The Private City: Philadelphia in Three Periods of Growth*, (Philadelphia: University of Pennsylvania Press) 1968, p. xii.

[219]Alexis de Tocqueville, *Democracy in America*, George Lawrence (tr.), (New York: Doubleday, Anchor) 1969, p. 287.

opinions and practices that create the moral fabric of a society. They are rooted in our religious tradition, our long experience of political participation and our economic life. If we are to better understand the appropriate role of economic institutions in the American tradition, then we must consider the relationships of economic, political and religious ideas and practices as well as the tensions that have developed among them.

Since colonial times, Americans have had a genuine desire to create a decent society for all. That concern was expressed in the idea of a convenant, so important to our Puritan ancestors, and reaffirmed in the Declaration of Independence with its pledge of "our lives, our fortunes and our sacred honor" for the common good. But we have also shown a vigorous individualism. The individual with his needs, desires and interests, particularly economic interests, was seen as almost the only good, and whatever social arrangements were necessary were to be worked out by contracts that maximized the interests of individuals. Our covenant heritage provided the context within which a contract could work, for only with the fundamental trust that the covenant fosters will contracts be honored. The American Constitution was hammered out in major part as an instrument that could balance the various conflicting interests threatening the stability of the nation, and use the energy of those interests to offset and check one another. John Adams pointed to the covenant context within which the Constitution was assumed to operate when he said during his first year as our first vice president: "We have no government armed with power capable of contending with human passions unbridled by morality and religion. Our Constitution was made only for a moral and a religious people. It is wholly inadequate to the government of any other."[220]

Adams tended to view virtue and interest as offsetting principles, both necessary to a republic. But Noah Webster spoke for many in describing the kind of economic interest that was essential. He wrote in 1787:

> *Virtue*, patriotism, or love of country, never has and never will be, till men's natures are changed, a fixed permanent principle and support of government. But in an agricultural country, a general possession of land in fee simple, may be rendered perpetual, and the inequalities introduced by commerce, are too fluctuating to endanger government. An equality of property, with a necessity of alienation, constantly operating to destroy combinations of powerful families, is the very *soul of a republic*.[221]

The idea was that an approximate equality of economic conditions was essential to the operation of free institutions, because economic equality and also economic independence is necessary for the creation of enlightened

---

[220]Quoted in John R. Howe, Jr., *The Changing Political Thought of John Adams*, (Princeton, N.J.: Princeton University Press) 1966, p. 185.

[221]Quoted in Gerald Stourzh, *Alexander Hamilton and the Idea of Republican Government*, (Stanford, Conn.: Stanford University Press) 1970, p. 230.

citizens. Alexander Hamilton expressed the common view when he said, "In the general course of human nature, a power over a man's subsistence amounts to a power over his will." Concentration of economic power, therefore, would create a degree of dependence for many that would be incompatible with their role as free citizens. Hamilton felt pessimistic that such concentrations of wealth could be avoided and so predicted the republican institutions in America would survive but briefly: "As riches increase and accumulate in few hands; as luxury prevails in society; virtue will be in a greater degree considered as only a graceful appendage of wealth, and the tendency of things will be to depart from the republican standard."[222]

Jefferson, characteristically, was more optimistic about the possible social and economic basis for American free institutions. He, like Noah Webster, looked above all to the independent farmer as the model of a good citizen. In his *Notes on the State of Virginia* he linked the religious, the political and the economic in his discussion of farmers:

> Those who labor in the earth are the chosen people of God, if He had a chosen people, whose breasts He has made His peculiar deposit for substantial and genuine virtue. It is the focus in which he keeps alive that sacred fire, which otherwise might escape from the face of the earth. Corruption of morals in the mass of cultivators is a phenomenon of which no age nor nation has furnished an example. It is the mark set on those, who, not looking up to heaven, to their own soil and industry, as does the husbandman, for their subsistence, depend for it on casualties and caprice of customers. Dependence begets subservience and venality, suffocates the germ of virtue, and prepares fit tools for the design of ambition.[223]

That the farmer was, like the merchant and the artisan, also finally dependent on the market, Jefferson chose for the moment to ignore, but it is clear that it is his relative autonomy that made the farmer the model citizen in a free republic.

For all the differences between them the founders of the republic had a fairly clear understanding of the interaction of economics, politics and religion in a republic. Great wealth and extreme poverty alike were to be avoided. They undermined morality and piety, so important for the social climate of free institutions, and they produced tyrannical attitudes on the one hand, and subservient ones on the other, that were equally incompatible with active citizenship.

De Tocqueville, writing about America in the 1830's, continued to raise the social and political issues that were of such concern to our founders. He worried lest too great a concern with economic prosperity undermine our

---

[222]Quoted in *Ibid.*, p. 71.

[223]From Query XIX of the *Notes on the State of Virginia* in *The Complete Jefferson*, Saul Padover, ed., (Duell, Sloan and Pearce) 1943, p. 678.

free institutions by drawing men's attention too exclusively to their private and selfish interests. Like John Adams he felt that the importance of religion in American life was a significant check on narrow self-interest. Like Jefferson he thought public participation was the best school of democratic citizenship. Like our founders, he believed that economic independence and social cooperation could go hand in hand in America. As de Tocqueville wrote:

> The free institutions of the United States and the political rights enjoyed there provide a thousand continual reminders to every citizen that he lives in society. At every moment they bring his mind back to this idea, that it is the duty as well as the interest of men to be useful to their fellows. Having no particular reason to hate others, since he is neither their slave nor their master, the American's heart easily inclines toward benevolence. At first it is of necessity that men attend to the public interest, afterwards by choice. What had become calculation becomes instinct. By dint of working for the good of his fellow citizens, he in the end acquires a habit and taste for serving them.[224]

Citizen Participation

De Tocqueville, then, in ways consistent with the beliefs of Jefferson and Adams, argued that the key to American democracy was active civic associations. He observed that only through active involvement in common concerns could the citizen overcome the sense of relative isolation and powerlessness that was a part of the insecurity of life in an increasingly commercial society. Associations, along with decentralized, local administration, were to mediate between the individual and the centralized state, providing forums in which opinion could be publicly and intelligently discussed and the subtle habits of public initiative and responsibility learned and passed on. Associational life, in de Tocqueville's thinking, was the best bulwark against the condition he feared most: the mass society of mutually antagonistic individuals who, once alienated, became prey to despotism. These intermediate structures might check, pressure and restrain the tendencies of centralized government to assume more and more administrative control.

What de Tocqueville sought, then, was a modern version of classic political democracy. He thought social differentiation inescapable, since the division of labor creates differences among groups in the goals they seek to attain. Democratic politics must seek to coordinate—and adjust—these differentiations in the interest of equity and concern for the liberty of all. Without those specific loyalties to community and function that the older religious tradition had identified as the sense of calling. de Tocqueville feared that the individual lost his sense of involvement and worth, and, literally, his identity as a citizen. On the other hand, without the wider

---

[224]De Tocqueville, *op. cit.*, pp. 512-513.

linkages political alliances provided, local and occupational groups were always prone to an exclusive narrowness antithetical to the universal ideals so indispensable to a modern democracy.

A vital democracy, then, requires a complex effort to achieve a political community through balancing the relationships among the administrative organization of the state, the individual citizen and the associations that come between individual and state.

Association does something more fundamental than accomplish the basic goal of providing the greatest happiness for the greatest number. It brings into being a political situation qualitatively different from that of individuals confronted by a bureaucracy of governmental control. By association individuals become citizens and thereby acquire a sense of personal connection and significance that is unavailable to the depoliticized, purely private person. Through mutual deliberation and joint initiative, moral relationships of trust and mutual aid are established and come to embody the meaning of citizenship for the individual.

Politics in the genuinely associational sense of substantially more than the pursuit of self-interest, since it involves sharing responsibility for acts that create a quality of life quite different from the mere sum of individual satisfactions. De Tocqueville hoped that civic participation could make the individual an active, politically aware subject rather than a passive object of state control. For de Tocqueville, lack of participation, no matter what its material effects, was humanly degrading and finally a manifestation of despotism. In this he was restating the traditional, and basic, civic republican notion that human dignity requires the freedom that exists and grows only in a context of active civic community. The uneven history of democratic participation in America since de Tocqueville's time has not contradicted this part of his message, though it is a goal American society has never fully experienced.

The Individual and the Community

In de Tocqueville's America, as for most Americans throughout the nineteenth century, the basic unit of association and the practical foundation of both individual dignity and participation was the local community. There a civic culture of individual initiative was nurtured through custom and personal ties inculcated by widely shared religious and moral values. Concern for economic betterment was strong but it operated within the context of a still functional covenant concern for the welfare of the neighbor. In the town the competitive individualism stirred by commerce was balanced and humanized through the restraining influences of a fundamentally egalitarian ethic of community responsibility These autonomous small-scale communities were dominated by an active middle class, the traditional citizens of a free republic, whose members shared similar economic and social positions and whose ranks the less affluent segments of the population aspired to enter, and often succeeded. Most men were self-employed, and many who worked for others were saving capital to launch themselves on enterprises of their own. Westward expansion, as de Tocqueville noted, reproduced this pattern of a decentralized, egalitarian democracy across our continent. American citizenship was anchored in the institutions of the face-to-face community— the neighborliness—of the town. Such communities provided the social basis of the new Republican Party in the 1850's, and Abraham Lincoln was perhaps their noblest representative.

Undemocratic America

De Tocqueville carefully noted two forms of socioeconomic organization that differed profoundly from this form of civilization—which he considered basic to American democracy—and threatened its continued existence. One was the slave society of the South, which not only treated blacks inhumanly but also, as de Tocqueville in ways quite similar to Jefferson noted, degraded whites as well, reducing them to something considerably less than autonomous, responsible citizens.

The second ominous social form was the industrial factories, evident at first in the Northeast, which concentrated great numbers of poor and dependent workers in the new burgeoning mill towns. Here de Tocqueville feared a new form of authoritarianism was arising that made petty despots out of owners and managers and reduced workers to substandard conditions incompatible with full democratic citizenship. Ironically, the traumatic civil war that destroyed slavery enormously furthered the growth of the industrial structures that so profoundly threatened the original American pattern of decentralized democratic communities.

A National Economy

By the end of the nineteenth century the new economic conditions fatally unbalanced the community pattern of American life. New technologies, particularly in transportation, communications and manufacturing, pulled the many quasi-autonomous local societies into a vast national market. Problems arising in this increasingly centralized and economically integrated society required the growth of the structures of central government, and steadily sapped the ability of local associations to deal with local problems. Under these conditions the very meaning of the traditional idea of American citizenship was called into question.

This shift in emphasis had a profound effect on the role of the individual in society. One response was to adapt to the new structures of centralized economic power by choosing a career whose rewards are wealth and power rather than a calling that provided status and meaning within a community of complementary callings. This shift was becoming evident by the mid-nineteenth century but has progressed enormously in the twentieth, and is now dominant. Virtually all Americans depend directly or indirectly for livelihood, information and, often, ideas and opinions, on great centralized and technologized organizations, and they identify themselves more by professional prestige and privilege than by community ties. The increasing uniformity of national life has developed concomitantly with the rise of a national pattern of social inequality that has replaced the more immediately perceived differentiations of the local community.

Thus, individual hopes for betterment have come to focus on climbing a status ladder of occupations, and increasingly, upon the progress of the national economy as a whole. Westward migration and the founding of new settlements that provided for ever more citizens the status of yeoman farmer have given way to expectations of rising income, higher occupational status and suburban living. The expansion of the national economic system has replaced the frontier as the locus of opportunity.

In modern American experience, constraints and social discipline such as tax paying, company loyalties and professional commonality have been increasingly justified because they are instrumental to individual security and advancement. Some measure of equality of opportunity seemed the appropriate and "American" way to democratize this new national society, but the focus has been on private, economic betterment, not on the quality of shared, public life.

These tendencies, which bear an all too close resemblance to de Tocqueville's fear that an exclusive concern with material betterment would lead America away from free citizenship and toward a form of what he called "soft despotism," have not gone unopposed. Some forms of opposition, like the efforts of the late-nineteenth-century Populists and, later, the Progressives, to defend the integrity of the local community, have failed, though even in failure they have presented examples of a citizenry that will not passively accept its fate.

Democracy at Work

Other efforts to control the most exploitative tendencies of the industrial sector, such as the enactment of health and safety laws and the regulation of working hours and minimum wages, have been more successful. The growth of labor unions has brought some sense of citizenship rights into the workplace. The tendencies toward despotism inherent in profit-oriented bureaucratic corporations have been muted at the bargaining table where wages, hours and working conditions as well as grievance procedures have all become subject to quasi-political negotiation. This has not, with minor exceptions, given the worker a say in the direction of the corporation that employs him, but it has given him some sense of active participation in the conditions of his employment and some protection against any tendency of his employers to disregard his needs.

In our recent history, significant social movements such as the Civil

Rights movement or the movement to oppose the Vietnam War have continued to have an impact on public policy. Such movements have mobilized large coalitions of people, motivated by a combination of self-interest and a great deal of disinterested civic concern, to a degree of participation in the political process not common in day-to-day political life. That such movements can still make a difference in our society, even though not as quickly or as completely as some would desire, is evidence that the civic republican spirit is still present among us.

Diluted Principles

Although the spirit of republican citizenship and the social conditions that support it are by no means gone from American life, alarming danger signals are visible. The belief in the individual as a self-interested "economic animal" is certainly not new in our history, but it is less and less tempered by the covenant values based in local communities and religious mores. Now, shorn of many of the nurturant values of traditional civic association, the ethos of self-advancement as an exclusive strategy has been able to run rampant with fewer constraints. The result has been a definition of personal worth almost exclusively in terms of competitive success, measured by status and advancement in large organizations. The ideals of loyalty and service based on personal trust and commitment have faltered in this atmosphere.

Even when the national economy was rapidly expanding and the hope of significant self-advancement was realistic, the social consequences were often what we have recently heard described as "moral malaise." Inability to commit oneself to or believe in anything that transcends one's private interests leads to a less positive commitment to family and community and a negative self-absorption and greed.

Unfortunately, the difficulties arising from too exclusive a concern with self-betterment have of late been enormously compounded by the gradually dawning knowledge that the cup of plenty is not inexhaustible. Material blessings were never shared equitably in America, but while the economy was growing everyone could look forward to more. However, if wealth is not going to grow or is going to grow much more slowly, and our values have become focused on self-interest, then we are on the verge of the war of all against all, as each interest group strives to get to the well first before it dries up.

The Role of Government

We have for a long time turned, not unwisely, to government to regulate the quest for economic aggrandizement. The ideology if radical individualism, with its notion that the pursuit of self-interest is the best incentive for a free society, has always required an umpire who will guarantee at least minimal conditions of fairness in the race for material goods. Government has been that umpire and has become increasingly active in that role in recent decades. While privileged individuals and groups have often viewed the role of government as intrusive and even destructive, less privileged groups have found in government a protector against the worst consequences of being crushed by the inequities of our competitive economy. The welfare program, with all its inadequacies, and affirmative action have brought a measure of justice to people who have been deprived and/or handicapped by poverty and prejudice. Perhaps it is a sign of the times that such minimal and basic human programs are viewed by the privileged as programs designed to victimize *them*.

Our present danger does not come from government as such, or from self-seeking individuals either, for that matter. The danger to our democratic institutions comes rather from the declining effectiveness of the intervening structures—the variety of civic associations—that serve to mediate between individual and state. It is those intermediate structures that encourage citizenship and provide the best defense against despotism, soft or hard. Without them the government, even when acting benevolently, may encourage a dependence and a lack of civic concern that play into the hands of authoritarianism. The danger increases when the economic pie is growing slowly and erratically, when the privileged are talking about "social discipline" while the deprived feel existent inequalities more keenly.

In the meantime, public cynicism about the modern American notion of pursuit of economic self-interest in the context of free enterprise, tempered by a degree of expert bureaucratic finetuning by the Federal Government, is growing. The failures of conventional economics to meet certain problems—inflation, slow economic growth and national concern about the energy crisis—have engendered widespread public disillusionment in government and business corporations alike. One form of this disillusionment is a growing cynicism and a tendency to "look out for number one," together with a deepening fear of one's fellow citizens. Such sentiments as these, republican theorists warn, are the preconditions of despotism.

Social Structures

But another response to the failures of the recent pattern of American political and economic life is to look to the possibility of the revival of our democratic civic culture and social structures, and above all the intermediate local and neighborhood associations that nurture them. There are many who view the present necessity—to rethink the notion that quantitative, undifferentiated economic development is the answer to all our problems—as a genuine opportunity to recover aspects of our public life that could never be fully absorbed into that pattern. They view the present challenge not with dismay but rather as a stimulus to become our true selves as a democratic society.

On both the right and the left of the political spectrum there is much talk of intermediate structures. Some use the language of participatory public life simply as a means to attack the growth of "big government" without a reasonable assessment of the social benefits government confers; one that *no other structure* in our society can presently provide. For such critics the ideal intermediate structure is the business corporation, which they believe should be freed from "government interference."

Others who talk about intermediate structures view business corporations as massive structures of bureaucratic power, largely unresponsive to citizen needs, and certainly not forums for civic participation and democratic debate. Or else they see business corporations as needing drastic reform before they can function as truly representative intermediate structures. At any rate, however important it may be to nurture religious, ethnic, neighborhood and other forms of civic association, it is the economic institutions that are the key to our present difficulties, and it is a new way of linking our economic life with our democratic values that is the key to their solution.

Let us consider the relevance of the early American pattern to our present situation. The founders saw occupation and economic condition as closely linked to the religious, social and political bases of a free society. They feared excessive wealth, excessive poverty and lack of independence in one's occupation. They thought self-employment the best guarantee of good citizenship, which would then lead to civic cooperation in the local community, particularly when nurtured by the religious and moral ideal of the covenant.

Our present circumstances—massive economic inter-dependence, employment mostly in large organizations and the near disappearance of the self-employed farmer, merchant and artisan—would seem so far from the vision of the founders as to have no connection with it. But if we consider the intentions and purposes of the founders, and not the economic conditions they found close at hand, then we might understand how their vision and wisdom could apply to our present situation.

If the intention of the founders was to create independent citizens who could then cooperate together in civic associations so as to produce a democratic society conducive to the dignity of all, we must consider how we might attain the same ends under the conditions of our present political economy. A renewed citizenship must build upon our still living traditions of volunteerism and cooperation wherever they may be found, but it cannot take the older forms and resources for granted. Contemporary citizenship requires a moral commitment as well as an institutional basis appropriate to our interdependent, occupationally segmented national society. And because professionalism and occupational identification have become so crucial to contemporary society and personal identity, a renewed civic identity must be institutionalized in the workplace as well as the community at large if we want to avoid the classic war of "all against all."

Private/Public Enterprise

If we would recover again the social and personal commitment to free institutions that is the life-blood of a democratic society, then we must bring the public democratic ethos into the sphere of economic life. To view economic institutions as "private" made sense when most Americans spent their lives on family farms or in family firms. But today when most American men and a rapidly increasing proportion of American women spend much of their lives in large economic structures that are for most purposes "public" except that the profits they make go to institutional and individual "private" stockholders—it becomes imperative to bring the forms of citizenship and of civic association more centrally into the economic sphere. There is no simple formula for achieving that end; it certainly does not require "nationalization," which, by bringing vast economic bureaucracies under the domination of the Federal Government, would make the democratization of economic life even more difficult. What we need is a series of experiments with new forms of autonomous or semi-autonomous "public enterprise" as well as reformed versions of "private enterprise" as we pursue, with circumspection, our aim of a healthy economy that is responsive to democratic values.

Two related problems inherent in our present "private" form of economic organization must be attended to if we would make ours a healthier democratic society: the profit imperative (the so-called tyranny of the bottom line), and bureaucracy as an organization form. During the long period of sustained and rapid economic growth the profit imperative may not have had entirely negative social consequences. An optimistic business climate allows a fair degree of experimentation that keeps employment high, and the trickle-down effect means that even those at the bottom of the economic ladder participate, if not equally then at least partially, in the overall economic growth. Even under such conditions there are problems that will be ignored because it is not maximally profitable in the short run to deal with them. For example, as long as we would buy cheap oil from the Near East there was little incentive to consider stringent measures of energy conservation. There will also be populations and regions that will be overlooked, and that will participate only slightly in the overall growth. Viable but minimally profitable enterprises for such groups may not be developed because more highly profitable investment opportunities exist elsewhere.

If the profit imperative creates problems even under "normal" conditions of economic growth, its consequences become severe under conditions of economic stringency. The experimentation and free-wheeling nature of a period of growth begins to close down because everything must be justified in terms of the bottom line. Social purposes and human needs—perhaps even the survival of some individuals—that cannot be translated into a short-term prospect of profitability are necessarily ignored. This is especially true if we analyze the impact of inflation on wage-earners in the basic necessities: health, energy, housing and food. It is under these conditions that a new, more public and more civic purpose must be injected into the economy and the language of "economic democracy" or "economic planning" comes into play. We will consider further what that language might mean after we look

114

at the second problematic feature of our present form of economy: its bureaucratic organization.

The Dynamics of Bureaucracy

Bureaucracy is in principle a highly efficient means of social organization in which large numbers of people can be mobilized to attain a given end. In a sense, an army is the archetypal bureaucracy. Decisions are made by a very small group at the top, and commands are transmitted to those below. Viewed in this light, bureaucracy would seem to be in principle anti-democratic; indeed despotism would seem to be its very essence. Under modern conditions bureaucracy, even military bureaucracy, seldom approaches such an authoritarian ideal type. In a large and highly differentiated organization where many individuals and groups have highly technical and managerial skills, they cannot simply be commanded but must be motivated, at least in part through some sense of participation in common projects and common ends. Of course, much of what appears to be a "democratic" aspect to bureaucratic organization may be human manipulation by those in charge. On the other hand it is clear that a large complex organization with rather specific ends cannot be organized like a town meeting. Not everyone can play an equal part in such an organization.

The profit imperative and the bureaucratic form of social organization often combine in an unfortunate way. The profit imperative itself can become a kind of tyrannical command that limits the options even of top management. Concerns for the humanization of the work process or more vigorous corporate social responsibility may have to be shelved under pressure to show profitability. Unfortunately, it is not true that all good things are "good business." If they were, our economy and our society would not be suffering their present difficulties. In any case it seems clear that a broadening of the purposes of economic organization to include a greater range of social responsibilities than the obligation to show a profit goes hand in hand with a concern to make the internal operation of economic organization more genuinely responsive to human needs.

Cooperatives and Non-Profit Corporations

This is not the place to more than hint at the possibilities for transforming our economy into a more democratic and socially responsible one. Clearly we have only begun to realize the values of consumer, publicly owned, or cooperative forms of economic enterprise. Where there is expert assistance and capital available, a variety of small-scale economic enterprises can be organized as self-help development efforts. Such ventures make excellent sense in economically depressed areas; they provide multiple opportunities for those otherwise excluded from employment. In addition to fostering the self-respect that comes from steady employment, the owners of a cooperative enterprise receive an education in the democratic process when they choose their board of directors and participate in a variety of functions in running their own business. Further, the cooperative is not tempted to drain the profits away from its own community as a branch of a large firm would do. Profits are ploughed back into local expansion, the proliferation of other cooperatives and, often, some forms of local social services, such as day-care centers, health clinics and credit unions.

The non-profit corporation has already proved its usefulness in the form of Community Economic Development Corporations (CDCs). By combining profitable or at least viable economic undertakings with a variety of community services, the non-profit corporation has many of the advantages of the cooperative on a larger scale. In some areas, such as the provision of health care, such groups such as the Laiser Permanente Health Maintenance Organization plan—may provide better care at less cost than either government or private medicine could do.

Experiments in Private/Public Enterprise

Undoubtedly we have only begun to realize the potential in a variety of forms public enterprise can take. The Tennessee Valley Authority, for all the opposition it has generated, stands as a reasonably successful venture in public enterprise. As economic difficulties beset some of our largest corporations, experiments with mixed public/private enterprise might be contemplated. The Chrysler Corporation, for example, in return for government economic backing, might be required to take public-consumer representatives onto its board of directors and to devote a significant part of its effort to the development of energy-efficient engines to cope with what can only be a continually deepening fuel crisis.

Experimentation can also occur within an organization. Some firms have for many years distributed stock in the company as a bonus to workers to make them part owners. Such a device brings the private corporation and the cooperative closer together. Experiments such as the one at the Harman autoparts plant in Bolivar, Tennessee, have brought management and the United Auto Workers together to improve and democratize the work process. General Motors has been more receptive to extensive cooperation with the UAW than have the other major automobile makers. Such experiments go beyond the provision of basic citizen rights to workers. Yet although they offer workers a more active participatory role, they still fall short of bringing workers into the decision-making process about the ends and purposes of the enterprise. Including employee representatives on boards of directors is one solution to that problem, but it does not entirely meet our present need. Since employees stand to profit from corporate aggrandizement, especially when they have an effective voice in the organization, they may be tempted by a collective egoism not morally superior to that of the "private" managers. Thus, especially where corporations are large and powerful and make decisions affecting very large numbers of people outside the organization, there is a real need for public and consumer as well as employee representatives on boards of directors.

Of course, all of these forms of experimentation are dependent on a climate of financial and government support. Capital at relatively modest rates of interest must be made available to cooperatives and other forms of public enterprise. There should be ways to make tax savings available to corporations that can show a consistent record of public responsibility at the cost of their own reduced profitability. A program of government grants might be made available to support innovative efforts to democratize the workplace, humanize work or heighten community responsibility. Particularly in a situation of little or no economic growth, the emphasis must shift from quantitative expansion to qualitative improvement. Only a generally favorable climate of public opinion and government policy would support the leaders and managers who want to move in these new directions. They are ready and able to help solve our problems, but need mature leadership with moral courage.

Even though the present failure of public courage may be discouraging, there are still some aspects of our present situation that could lead to a reinvigoration of our mores and a new sense of the importance of the covenant model to balance the present dominance of the contract model. The greatest opportunity exists in the growing realization that endless—and mindless— economic growth is not the answer to all our problems, even if it were possible. And we are only beginning to comprehend some of the inherent brutalities of an over-technologized society. If the rise of industrial capitalism, for all the material benefits it has conferred, also lies at the root of most of our problems, then the faltering of the economy that has become evident since the early 1970's, and that shows no early sign of change, may provide an occasion for some profound reflections about the direction of America in the decades ahead. If serious Americans in large numbers realize that the cause of our difficulties is not "big government" but, rather, a way of life that worships wealth and power, that makes economic profit the arbiter of all human values and that delivers us into the tyranny of the bottom line, then it may be possible to re-examine our present institutions and the values they embody.

A democratization of our economic institutions, by whatever name, is a key to the revitalization of our mores and our public life. Clearly the fusion of economic and governmental bureaucracies into a kind of superbureaucracy is not the answer, but would only compound the causes of our difficulty. The crisis in confidence that has overtaken our present system of bureaucratic capitalism can lead to a new shared public authority in our economic life.

We must develop the conditions for a new, shared public authority through a movement for the reform of economic life. The process needs to invite the enclaves of neighborly cooperation out from their present defensive position on the peripheries of our public life to join in a larger effort to transform the mainstream institutions into vehicles for and expressions of citizen concern and positive values. This necessitates a process of moral education at the same time it attempts to restructure institutions. It aims to decentralize where that makes sense; to include the participation of many of those—women, minorities, the elderly, youth and the poor—who have long been left out; to provide a broadly representative collegial leadership from which executive management can take its cue; and to empower citizens by providing experience in civic life. All this is quite different from a simplistic strategy that would "upgrade" the disadvantaged to share the exclusive and private vision of competitive advancement often promoted by corporate ideology. Rather, the effects of such a positive movement, already beginning in many areas, would be to revitalize the principle of civic association, to strengthen the intermediate structures that make it possible for individual citizens to maintain their independence and to make their voices heard, and, thus, to reinforce the vitality of our free institutions generally. Moving into a world of little or no economic growth, without such a process of democratic character and values, would only precipitate no-win Hobbesian struggles among groups wanting to profit at one another's expense—a struggle already too evident in our present politics of special interests.

But a healthy shift in the organization of our economic life, with all it would entail in our society, cannot be expected as a result of mere technocratic or organizational manipulation. So great a change, overcoming not only entrenched power but entrenched ways of thinking, could be brought about only by a change in social or moral consciousness. We are, like it or not, going to face a world of increasing scarcity and simplicity, voluntary or involuntary. We can enter that world with bitterness and antagonism, with a concern to protect ourselves and our families whatever the consequences to others. Or we can enter it with a renewed sense of what John Winthrop meant when said in 1630, "We must delight in each other, make others' conditions our own, rejoice together, mourn together, labor and suffer together, always having before our eyes . . . our community as members of the same body."

To come to terms with what has happened to us in the last century in a way that allows us to regain the moral meaning and the public participation that characterized our formative period—that seems the only way to create a liveable society in the decades ahead. There are no easy formulas as to how to attain that goal. A great deal of creative experimentation and a variety of types of organization that will explore different possibilities are surely needed. But only the presence of a new sense of moral commitment and human sensibility can provide the time and space for such experimentation.

Summary

It would seem clear that though the rise of coporate capitalism has brought

Americans many good things, it has also disrupted our traditional social system while finally creating enormous economic problems that it cannot seem to solve. The national private economy has not only created problems but has, through its enormous political influence, involved government and massive government spending in ways that have been self-serving and thus compounded those problems.

Ever since World War II, high-technology and service industries have boomed in the "sun belt" with the help of massive military orders and huge Federal underwriting for infra-structure. During the same years the industrial cities of the Northeast and Midwest have been allowed to deteriorate. Profits have been enormous, but the human costs have been very high; New York, Cleveland and Youngstown are the most vivid examples of the general trend. It has been suggested that this unbalanced pattern of growth and stagnation will exact enormous sums in taxpayers' money in the decades ahead. It could have been avoided if the public interest had been given greater consideration in the planning of a healthy and balanced national economy.

Another example of the disastrous consequences of economic decisions made solely on the basis of profitability is the proliferation of energy-consuming, pollution-creating automobile and truck transportation at the expense of rapid transit and railroad systems, especially since World War II. Due to the power of automobile and oil lobbies, billions have been spent in Federal highway programs while railroad and mass transit supports have been attacked as "wasteful." Dependence in initially cheap foreign oil, which was part of this transportation package, has proved to be not only an economic time-bomb but an international political disaster that has made our national interest highly vulnerable.

Our pattern of unbalanced economic growth, its delayed costs and our dependence on foreign oil have contributed greatly to our present high inflation rate, which, as we pointed out in the beginning of this chapter, is our most serious immediate economic problem. It has become increasingly clear that we cannot come to terms with the causes of inflation or with inflation itself without planning on a scale that is unprecedented in America. Some learned economists suggest that only permanent wage-price controls will bring inflation under control, but if and when that occurs, such controls will be effective only in the context of a structure of general economic planning. Stephen A. Marglin, Professor of Economics at Harvard University, recently wrote:

> The real issue of the 1980's is not planning, but what kind of planning. If planning is to be democratic in process and end product, the entire structure of the capitalist economy must be overhauled to become significantly more participatory, from the shop floor to the corporate board room.
>
> Either our dominant economic institution, the corporation, will come to reflect democratic ideals, or the polity will come increasingly to incorporate the notion of the divine right of capital.

119

My own position is clear. Authoritarian capitalism is no longer a vehicle of human progress, but an obstacle. By contrast, democracy, extended to our economic institutions, has a rich and glorious future.[225]

Professor Marglin, as our historical review has shown, sets the issue in terms thoroughly consonant with our American democratic tradition.

In dealing with our economic problems, then, we must not be oriented to technical efficiency alone; that could produce an authoritarian solution. The economy is part—a central part—of our entire social system. That means that the criterion of success cannot be cost-accounting alone. The human implications of various forms of organization must always be considered. Above all, the economy must reinforce, not undermine, that structure of intermediate associations upon which the vitality of our democracy rests. Only an economy that can provide security, dignity, equality of opportunity and participation to all our citizens will be a democratic economy.

The Council believes that we have in America the human and natural as well as cultural and spiritual values to surmount the present challenges and reinvigorate our democratic life. We believe this is the true challenge of the eighties.

---

[225]Stephen A. Marglin, "Resolution for the '80s," *Harvard Magazine*, January–February 1980, pp. 23–24, with omissions.

ARTHUR I. BLAUSTEIN, Chairman
Berkeley, California

Mr. Blaustein is Director of the National Economic Development and Law Center, a public-interest law and planning center that provides assistance—throughout the country—to Legal Services attorneys and to low-income community organizations in the fields of community and economic development. He was Chairman of the Board of Directors of the Center for Rural Studies and is a member of the editorial board of *Social Policy* and *The Reporter*. Mr. Blaustein was Chairman of the Government Reorganization Task Force of the National Coalition of Neighborhood Organizations and also serves on the advisory board of Advocates for Women, and on the board of the National Commission on Law, Social Action and Urban Affairs of the American Jewish Congress.

Mr. Blaustein has been actively involved in antipoverty efforts since the original Economic Opportunity Act and served as Director of Legislative and Public Affairs, as well as Director of Inter-Agency Coordination and Inter-Governmental Affairs, for the U.S. Office of Economic Opportunity (Northeast Region).

He was associate editor of *War/Peace Report*, a journal of international law. He is the co-author of *The Star-Spangled Hustle* (Doubleday) and the author of *Man Against Poverty: World War III* (Random House), as well as numerous articles on issues of public policy for *Harper's, Saturday Review, Urban Affairs, The Nation, New Spirit* and other national magazines.

Mr. Blaustein received his M.A. in Public Law from Columbia University.

HANNAH HUME BAIRD
Florence, Kentucky

Mrs. Baird has served on the Human Services Advisory Board of the Northern Kentucky Area Development District, was co-founder and charter Chairperson of the Northern Kentucky Women's Political Caucus and has been an Associate Chairman of the Northern Kentucky YMCA Capital Funds Drive. She is past president of the Boone County Cancer Society, a co-founder and charter officer of the Woodspoint Nursing Home Auxillary and a member of the William Booth Salvation Army Hospital Auxillary.

A former teacher, Mrs. Baird is active in numerous other civic endeavors including the PTA and the Florence Woman's Club, and serves as a volunteer with the Daniel Boone Career Development Center, a division of the Kentucky Department of Corrections.

Mrs. Baird was appointed to the Kentucky Commission on Women by Governor Julian Carroll. Currently, she serves as Vice-Chairperson of the Northern Kentucky Human Services Planning Council, Chairperson of the Boone County Human Needs Assessment and Implementation Committee, a member of the Advisory Council to the President of the Northern Kentucky University Foundation, a member of the Executive Council of the Community Chest of the Greater Cincinnati Area and a member of the Northern Kentucky Area Development District Economic Development Commission.

In 1978 Mrs. Baird was honored by the *Cincinnati Enquirer* as one of the Ten Women of the Year from the areas of Southern Ohio, Southern Indiana and Northern Kentucky.

IRVING BLUESTONE
Detroit, Michigan

Mr. Bluestone, long active in labor contract negotiations and administration, is Vice President of the International Union of the United Auto Workers and Director of the UAW's General Motors Department. He is also Director of UAW's Michigan Community Action Program and has served as a member of numerous community and national organizations and on several commissions to which he was appointed by the President of the United States or the Governor of Michigan.

Mr. Bluestone currently serves on the Board of Directors of the Work in America Institute, the Executive Committee of the National Committee for Full Employment, the Board of Trustees of the German Marshall Fund of the United States, the Michigan State Housing Development Authority, the Board of Directors of the United Fund, the National Trade Union Council for Human Rights, the Advisory Committee of the Archives of Labor History and Urban Affairs of the Wayne State University, and the Board of Directors of the Health Care Institute of the Wayne State University. He is also Co-Chairman of the Michigan Quality of Worklife Council.

He is a graduate of the City College of New York, and his post-graduate studies were at the University of Bern in Switzerland.

In his 38-year career with the UAW, he has held many positions, first at the local union level, then as International Representative and as Administrative Assistant to a Vice President and to former UAW President Walter Reuther.

WILLIAM M. DALEY
Chicago, Illinois

Mr. Daley is an attorney and an associate member of the law firm of Daley,

Reilly and Daley and a partner of the Daley and Daley insurance firm. He is a member of the American, Illinois and Chicago Bar Associations, and the Chicago Board of Underwriters. Mr. Daley has been an active participant in numerous civic and social-service endeavors. He serves as the Director of the Chicago Convention and Tourism Bureau, and is a member of the St. Ignatius Benefit Committee and the Edgewood Community Association.

L.C. DORSEY
Jackson, Mississippi

Ms. Dorsey is the Associate Director of Southern Coalition on Jails and Prisons, a nine-state prison reform program. She is also Program Director for the Delta Ministry, a 15-year old, statewide, church-sponsored human rights organization.

She was formerly the Administrative Director of the Mississippi Prisoner's Defense Committee and also the Director of Social Services of Washington County Opportunities, Inc. Ms. Dorsey also served as director, coordinator and organizer of an agricultural cooperative serving 800 families in Bolivar County. She is a member of the National Association of Black Social Workers, the Mississippi Conference of Social Welfare and the Resolution Committee of the Southern Regional Council. Ms. Dorsey is the recipient of numerous awards including Woman of the Year of the Utility Club of New York, a Meritorious Service Award in self-help poverty programs from the Woman's Auxillary of the National Medical Association and two fellowships from the Black Women's Community Development Foundation.

Ms. Dorsey is in demand as lecturer on campuses and as a trainer in many human service programs.

The mother of six children, Ms. Dorsey is a member of the New Bethel M.B. Church, and writes articles on a free-lance basis for the *Jackson Advocate* and other publications.

HAZEL N. DUKES
Roslyn Heights, New York

Ms. Dukes is President of the New York State Conference of the National Association for the Advancement of Colored People, the second woman to hold that position. She also is the Director of Administrative Services for the New York City Off-Track Betting Corporation and a member of the Board of Directors of the Center for Women in Government, the Family Services Association of Nassau County, the North Hempstead Community Development Agency, the Roslyn Day Care Center and the Economic Opportunity Commission of Nassau County.

Ms. Dukes has received numerous awards from civic and community groups including the New York City Opportunities Industrialization Center, the National Association of Negro Business and Professional Women, the Economic Opportunity Commission of Nassau County, Inc., and the 1977 Social Action Award of the Nassau Alumnae Chapter of Delta Sigma Theta Sorority.

RUBY DUNCAN
Las Vegas, Nevada

Ms. Duncan is the Executive Director of Operation Life, Inc., a Community Development Corporation, and President of the Clark County Welfare and Economic Rights Organization. She serves on the Board of Directors of a number of community and national organizations including the Nevada Health Care Corporation, the Clark County Economic Opportunity Board, the Nevada State Advisory Council for Vocational-Technical Education, the Southern Nevada Human Relations Board, the National Organization for Women, the Western Association for Neighborhood Health Centers and the National Women's Lobby.

Ms. Duncan served as a consultant to the National Legal Aid Dependent Association and the National Health Law Project, and has been a delegate to the World conference for Peace in Moscow and the International Women's Year in Mexico City.

A mother of seven, Ms. Duncan has been cited by *McCall's* for her significant contributions to her country, and in 1974 was named the Outstanding Afro-American of Las Vegas.

GEOFFREY FAUX
Whitefield, Maine

Mr. Faux, an economist, is Co-Director of the Exploratory Project for Economic Alternatives, a foundation-supported research and public education program developing alternative proposals and strategies for strengthening equal opportunity and democracy in the American economy.

He has been an economic consultant to community organizations, government agencies and business corporations, has served on the boards of several antipoverty organizations and has been active in various low-income housing, consumer and economic development projects.

Mr. Faux has been Director of the Office of Economic Development of the U.S. Office of Economic Opportunity, and Director of the Center for Community Economic Development in Cambridge, Massachusetts. He headed the Task Force on Community Development for the Twentieth Century Fund, and has worked as an economist with the U.S. Departments of State, Commerce and Labor. Mr. Faux has been a lecturer at Harvard University, Harvard Law School, Yale Law School, Massachusetts Institute of Technology, Bowdoin College and a number of state universities.

He is the author or co-author of articles that have appeared in a variety of anthologies, newspapers and periodicals, including *The New York Times, The New Republic, Social Policy* and *The Progressive.* He co-authored *The Star-Spangled Hustle* (Doubleday), and wrote *New Hope for the Inner City* (20th Century Fund).

EDWARD F. FEIGHAN
Cleveland, Ohio

Mr. Feighan is a County Commissioner for Cuyahoga County, Ohio.

He served six years in the Ohio House of Representatives, where he distinguished himself in the fields of low- and moderate-income housing and juvenile justice. While a member of the House, Mr. Feighan completed law school, receiving his Juris Doctor from Cleveland-Marshall College of Law.

As a County Commissioner, Mr. Feighan was the primary overseer of the reorganization designed to make the County's human services programs more responsive to citizens' needs; he also achieved improvements in the services for abused children.

Mr. Feighan is a member of many local service organizations and has received numerous civic and community awards.

LINDA HADLEY
Chinle, Navaho Nation (Arizona)

Mrs. Hadley is Assistant Director of the Navaho Mental Health Program at the Rough Rock Demonstration School.

A bilingual, bicultural specialist, she has also served as liaison for the various communities within the Navaho Nation.

Mrs. Hadley has been Secretary of the Community Action Committee of the Forest Lake-Kitsillee Chapters, Navaho Nation, and is a member of the Board of the Office of Navaho Economic Opportunity, Fort Defiance, Navaho Nation, and the Board of Directors of the Dineh Cooperatives at Chinle.

JUAN JOSE MALDONADO
San Juan, Texas

Mayor Maldonado has been Chief Executive Officer of San Juan, Texas, since April 1977. A former teacher and education supervision specialist, he has been a consultant on bilingual and bicultural education, migrants and vocational education, drug education, parental involvement in schools, and psychological evaluation.

Mayor Maldonado serves as Chairman of the Board of the Rio Grande Valley Development Company and is a charter member of the Pan American University Alumnae Association. He also is a member of the Texas Association for Bilingual Education, the Texas Personnel and Guidance Association and the Texas State Teachers Association, and has served on the boards of directors of the San Juan Boys Club, the Hidalgo County Health Care Corporation and the Credit Committee of the Amigos Unidos Federal Credit Union of San Juan.

CHRISTINE PRATT-MARSTON
Lynnwood, Washington

Ms. Pratt-Marston is a consultant to the Project on Women and Mental Health of the University of Washington's School of Social Work. She was Director of the first licensed infant day-care program in Washington state; served as the Operation and Support Service Manager for Seattle Child

Care (Model Cities); was Director of the Seattle-King County Child Care Co-ordinating Committee; and served as a Social Welfare Specialist for Neighbor-hood House, which sponsored programs in housing projects throughout Seat-tle and King County. Ms. Pratt-Marston has provided training and technical assistance for Head Start and Community Action groups and has worked with welfare rights groups across the country. She has long been active as an expert and consultant about public policy issues affecting women, poverty, day care, child development, parent education, welfare reform and child advocacy, and for three years she was a consultant to Abt Associates, a Cambridge-based con-sulting and research firm, for the National Day-Care Study.

Ms. Pratt-Marston is currently Co-Chair of the National Organization for Women's Committee on Women and Poverty and a board member of the Na-tional Anti-Hunger Coalition as well as a member of numerous national and local human services organizations. She has served on the boards of the Family Counseling Services, the National Parents Federation for Day Care and Child Development, the Puget Sound Comprehensive Health Planning Council, the King County Child Care Coordinating Committee and the Welfare Reform Steering Committee. As a disabled single parent of four children, during the past ten years she has intermittently received Aid to Families with Dependent Children.

W. PHILIP McLAURIN
Portland, Oregon

Mr. McLaurin, Director of the Urban Crime Prevention Program of ACTION, was ombudsman for the State of Oregon. As the Acting Director of the Training and Employment Division of Portland, he was responsible for the planning, operating and monitoring of the city's $24-million Comprehensive Employment and Training Act (CETA) program. He has also been Executive Assistant to the Mayor of Portland.

A consultant to institutions of higher learning on the organization and development of Afro-American studies, Mr. McLaurin has been an Assistant Professor of Afro-American Studies at Smith College, and Director of the Black Studies Center and Chairman of the Black Studies Program at Portland State University. An expert on youth activities and community organizations, he has served as Director of the Portland Metropolitan Youth Commission summer youth programs and the Citizens' Information Center of Chester, Pennsylvania.

Mr. McLaurin is a member of the Board of Directors of the Oregon Devel-opment Disabilities Advocacy Center, the Martin Luther King, Jr., Scholar-ship Fund of Oregon and the Executive Board of the Tri-Community Council. He is a member of the Albina Voter Registration and Education Committee and the NAACP, and a former member of the American Association of University Professors, the Oregon State Board of Higher Education and the Board of Directors of the Parry Center. His honors include selection as an Outstanding Young Man in America by the National Junior Chamber of Commerce and a listing in *Who's Who in Black America.*

HENRY M. MESTRE, JR.
Oakland, California

Mr. Mestre is Executive Director of the Spanish Speaking Unity Council, a Community Development Corporation in Oakland. He has served the Unity Council since 1968 in positions such as Director for Community Services, Program Developer, Education Specialist and Employment Security Trainer. Mr. Mestre is a member of the Private Industry Council and the Overall Economic Development Planning Committee of the City of Oakland. He also serves on the Board of Governors of the Opportunity Funding Corporation and the Board of Directors of the California Federation for Technology and Resources and the New Oakland Committee.

Mr. Mestre has served on the Education Committee of the Alameda County Health Planning Council, the San Francisco Bay Area Council and on several Advisory Committees to the Oakland Schools. A graduate of University of California, Berkeley, Mr. Mestre received the Master of Business Administration from Pepperdine University in 1980.

EVELYN WATTS
St. Petersburg, Florida

Mrs. Watts, a retired nurse, is active in community projects relating to the problems of the poor and minorities. She is a member of the County Board of the National Association for the Advancement of Colored People, the Council for Human Relations, the Executive Committee of the Gulf Coast Legal Services Corporation, the Community Improvement Projects Committee of St. Petersburg, the Governor's Nursing Home Ombudsman Committee, and the Pinnelas County Opportunity Council.

The recipient of numerous civic and community awards, Mrs. Watts has served as a member of the Board of the Gulf Coast Health Systems, the Silver Haired Legislature, the League of Women Voters, the South Pinnelas Senior Citizens Group and Module 16, which advises the City of Saint Petersburg on the use of Federal funds for depressed areas.